Diving & Snorkeling Guide to
Palau
and
Yap

By TIM ROCK

2016 Edition

German Channel, Palau

Yap manta ray

About the Author:

Tim Rock is an internationally published photojournalist who specializes in the ocean realm. Based on Guam in the Western Pacific Ocean, Rock has traveled Micronesia, the Indo-Pacific and worldwide for three decades. He is the author of numerous Lonely Planet Diving & Snorkeling guides, produced the ACE award finalist Aquaquest Micronesia Television series and has won awards from the AP, UPI and NPPA for writing and photography. His website: **timrock.photoshelter.com**

Acknowledgements

A special thanks to Francis Toribiong, founder of Fish N Fins in Palau, who has been a great supporter, a co-author of past guides and has shared many Palau adventures with me over the years. Thanks to Sam Scott who has been a strong supporter of many of my personal projects in Palau. And to Bill and Patricia Acker of Yap's Manta Ray Resort who have been good for Micronesia and Yap diving and conservation.

Photographic Equipment Used

Rock uses Aquatica underwater housings with Ikelite strobes and TLC arms. He uses Nikon cameras with Nikon, Sigma, Tokina and Tamron lenses.

Main Modeling - Yoko Higashide & Natalia Baechtold. Additional modeling - Ai Futaki, Elaine Kwok, Leah Asanuma, Laura Luedke and Stefanie Brendl.
© 2016 by Tim Rock/Doubleblue.com and Mantaraypublishing.com

Palau Rock Islands

Traditional Yap dance

Diving & Snorkeling Guide to
Palau and Yap

Contents	Page
Overview of Palau	6
Geography/Fauna	8
History	11
Culture	13

Practicalities

Climate/Language	14
Getting There	14
Getting Around	15
Entry & Exit	15
Palau Visitor Info	15
Departure Tax	16
Time	16
Telecommunications/Postal	16
Electricity	17
Weights & Measures	17
What to Bring	17
UW Photography	17
Diving Permits	18
Accommodations/Dining	18
Shopping	19
Diving Permits	19
Activities & Attractions	21
Palau Snorkeling	22
Diving Health Safety	23
Dive Map	24

The Sites

North

1) Silvertip City (Ngeurangel Reef)	25
2) Kyangel Atoll (Ngcheangel Islands)	28
3) Devilfish City	29
4) Ngeremlengui Channel (West Passage)	32
5) Satan's Corner	34
6) Patrol Boat 31	35
6A) CH 26	37
7) Kibi Maru	38
8) The Seaplanes	39

Central

9) Short Dropoff	40
10) Tim's Reef	40
11) Teshio Maru	41
12) Jake Floatplane	42
13) Chandelier Cave	43
14) Ryuku Maru	44
15) Amatsu Maru (Black Coral Wreck)	44
16) Chuyo Maru	45
17) Helmet Wreck	46
18) Bottom Time Bar	48
19) Kesebekuu Channel (Lighthouse)	49
20) Iro Maru	50
21) Gozan Maru	52
22) Ulong Channel	53

Palau's natural arch

23) Siaes Tunnel	55		**YAP**		3) Yap Caverns	89		
24) Jellyfish Lake	56		Overview: Yap	80	4) Gilman Wall	91		
					5) Magic Kingdom	92		
			Practicalities		6) Spanish Walls	93		
South					7) Cherry Blossom Wall	95		
			Geography	83	8) Vertigo	97		
25) Shark City	58		Climate	83				
26) Ngerchong Dropoff	59		Getting There	84	The Mantas & Miil	99		
27) German Channel	60		Getting Around	84				
28) Big Dropoff	61		Entry	84	The Channels	100		
29) Turtle Wall	62		Health	84	9) Yap Corner	101		
30) New Dropoff	63		Time	84	Photographing Mantas	103		
31) Blue Corner	64				10) Spaghetti Factory	104		
Blue Corner Images	66		Electricity	85	11) Manta Ridge	107		
32) Blue Holes	70		Weights	85	12) Deep Cleaning			
33) Barnum Wall	71				Station	109		
34) Turtle Cove	72		Dive Equipment	85	13) Stammitsch	111		
35) Ngercheu Garden	73		Money & Credit Cards	85	14) Gofnuw	112		
(Matthew's Place)					15) Slow & Easy	113		
36) Peleliu Wall and Tip	74		Dive Site Map - Yap	86	16) Rainbow Reef	114		
37) Yellow Wall	75							
38) Peleliu Express	76		Diving in Yap	87	Palau Southwest Isles	116		
39) Angaur Point	77		Walls and Reefs	87	Yap Outer Carolines	117		
(Statue Point)			1) Gilman Tip	87				
Full Moon Fever	78		2) Lionfish Wall	88	Island Images	120 -124		

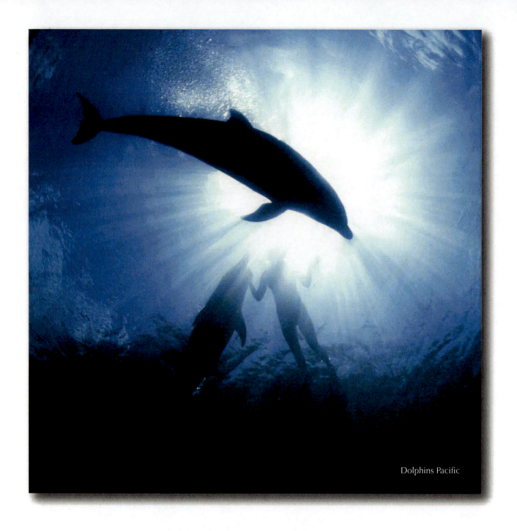

Dolphins Pacific

Overview: Palau

Palau may be the best known and most popular diving destination in Micronesia. Located about 800 miles southwest of Guam in the northwest Pacific Ocean, this is a vast, 100 mile long archipelago sitting in one of the richest locations in the ocean realm. Not only is its sea life abundant, its islands are home to exotic birds, wild monkeys and graceful flying foxes.

The land also is greatly varied. It comprises high-forested islands, sparkling coral atolls and stunning rock islands surrounded by a fringing of coral reef. Palau offers superb diversity ranging from tiny dots of land to hulking Babeldaob, the second largest island in Micronesia.

Once a well-kept secret by adventurous divers, Palau is now established as one of the most alluring and unique visitor destinations in the

Palau is called Rainbow's End

western Pacific.

    Near the center of the country are the emerald colored, jungled Rock Islands. These magnificent mushroom-like formations provide a maze of splendid natural beauty and a protected haven for many rare forms of sea life. Palau's waters support huge sea animals like the whale shark and the saltwater crocodile. It also hosts a wide spectrum of fish and coral life. With such diversity, virtually every dive promises something new and breathtaking.

The people of Palau are perhaps among the best-traveled and most adventurous of any culture in the Pacific. Seeking education, employment and adventure, many Palauans live or have lived elsewhere in the world only to return home for the betterment of their island home. Palauans are also very curious about other cultures and accepting of visitors. This makes Palau a unique place to visit. Palauans are generally incredibly quick to converse, joking and quipping.

Ngaardmau Falls

The population is still fairly small, around 20,000 people. This comprises mostly Palauans, but there are also many Filipino workers now living in Palau. Taiwanese, Japanese, Americans, Micronesians, Indonesians and some Europeans are also found here, making Palau an interesting melting pot.

Geography & Flora/Fauna

Palau is considered one of the world's natural wonders both above and below the surface of the water. Its immense barrier reef and broad landmass boast the second largest island in Micronesia next to Guam.

Palau is blessed with a rich diversity of biologically unique plants and animal life. Tropical forest covers much of the islands, including ironwood, banyan, coconut, pandanus and broadleaf hardwood trees. Other areas feature mangrove forest and even grassland savanna. Palau has 50 species of resident birds including seabirds, land and wetland varieties. The spectacular marine environment boasts over 1,500 species of fish, over 700 species of coral and anemones and even saltwater riparian crocodiles. This species of saltwater crocodile also

Rock Island snorkeling

common to Papua New Guinea.

Rare species such as giant Tridacna clam and dugongs (fluke-tailed sea cows) are also found here. There are no poisonous animals or reptiles on Palau, except a rarely seen jungle snake. Mammals are mostly introduced species, including monkeys brought in by the Germans to Angaur. There are lots of reptiles, including the crocodiles, geckoes and skinks, monitor lizards, two kinds of snakes and some large toads are found. Insect life is also diverse. There are no malarial mosquitoes here, but dengue fever is a problem so use repellent at night.

First birth ceremony

The islands represent two geologic happenings. The largest islands were formed by Eocene volcanic activity and comprise basalt and andesite. They have a high profile with an intricate stream system and a great diversity of plant life. The jungle is thick. In some places in Palau's interior it is impossible to penetrate. There is a freshwater lake in Babeldaob.

The Rock Islands are of limestone formation. Peleliu and Angaur are low platform and reef islands. Kyangel to the north is a classic coral atoll. The Southwest Islands comprise reef flats that have been subject to uplift.

Palau's marine life is almost unparalleled in the world. Its great diversity, combined with the varied terrain, has caused it to be named as one of the seven underwater wonders of the world by CEDAM International.

History

Historically, the early Palauans lived an isolated existence. The islands were rich in resources and the Palauans practiced terrace farming as well as fishing and hunting. Remains of the ancient terraces can still be seen on many Palauan hillsides today. It is believed that because the islands were so abundant, the Palauans had much time to practice artistic skills, perfect building practices, get into politics and even war with one another.

Two different chiefs have traditionally ruled the north and south of the islands. That is still true to this day, as traditional titles are still held by individuals and clans.

Babeldaob, the name for the northern large island, means "upper ocean" and Iouldaob, the name for southern Palau,

Japanese locomotive in Ngaardmau

Peleliu

means "lower ocean".

The actual origin of the first Palauans is uncertain, but linguistic and archaeological studies show that Malays from Indonesia, Melanesians from New Guinea and some Polynesians formed the basic genetic stock, resulting in a diversity of complexion and facial types. Palauan money consisting of yellow and orange glass beads, similar to money found in Indonesia, further traces the origin of Palauans to the Malay region.

Ancient village sites on the Rock Islands and the spectacular terraces on Babeldaob have been carbon dated to 1000BC. Further studies have also confirmed that the Palauan population before European contact was much larger than at any time.

Historians estimate there were 40,000 Palauans living in the islands at the time of first European contact when Capt. Henry Wilson shipwrecked the Antelope on Ulong Island in 1783. The islanders lived in a thriving and complex society that was highly organized. Still true today, women had an important advisory role and influential control over land and money.

The British controlled trade with the island until 1885, then the Spanish took over until 1899. Christianity became a strong influence in Palauan lives.

European diseases also took their toll. The population dwindled during the next century. Sadly, by 1900 there were only 4,000 Palauans left.

The Germans bought Palau and the rest of the Caroline Islands after Spain lost the Spanish-American War in 1899. German administrators introduced methods for stemming the diseases which was a Godsend to the decimated Palauans.

Japan & the War Years

Japan took control of the islands in 1914 and ruled them until the end of World War II. They built the islands into progressive and productive communities that specialized in mining, agriculture and fisheries. When the war came, the islands were also heavily fortified militarily.

The islands of Angaur and Peleliu were the settings for fierce battles; the one on tiny Peleliu lasting for three bloody months. A two-day air strike months before had sunk a major block of the Japanese fleet. War remnants still exist today.

Koror was wiped out after the U.S. forces took control of the islands. The job of rebuilding the intricate and productive Japanese infrastructure

Traditional Palauan dance

continues today, as the United States assumed a very passive role in administering the islands through the past four decades. The older people of Palau speak Japanese and sing Japanese songs when reminiscing.

Palau today is independent, working with a compact of free association with the United States. Thus, U.S. currency, the U.S. postal system and other minor support is still in use in Palau. The government attempts to govern its people and retain traditional values and roles by melding them with todays' progressive thoughts and politics.

Culture

Native Palauans have lived in the archipelago since 1000BC and in that time have developed a distinct culture. It expresses itself in its dance, music, myths and legends, depicted in intricately carved wooden storyboards and delicate woven artifacts. The abai or public meeting house, is still found in Koror, Kayangel and Airai. These structures offer tantalizing insights into Palauan society in the painted stories on interior posts, beams and gables.

By the time of European discovery in 1783, Palauans already exhibited a complex and sophisticated organization. The basis of Palauan society in general was centered on one theme: competition for money, prestige and power, the main thrust for which was political power within a clan or village. From an early age competition was characteristic of social life and Palauans channeled it into activities such as sports, politics and war.

The culture today is a mixture of old and new cultural, environmental, technological and political practices. Palau moves positively into the millenium with an increased emphasis on its number one business, tourism.

Western sunset

Climate

Palau's location: 7-30 north latitude, 133-30 east longitude makes it a very tropical place. Travel bringing only light clothing. It never gets cold in Palau, so only lightweight clothing is best. Bring a rain slicker and a light parka to have available on the boat as a cool rain after a dive can chill the diver.

Diving is year 'round. Rainy season is September through November, with showers possible starting in June. The trade winds blow starting in January, usually ending by May, with most dive sites sheltered by the islands. Temperatures vary from 76 at night to possible highs of 90 during the day, the average being around 86 degrees.

Attire is very casual and formal wear is considered unnecessary. Hats, sunglasses and high factor sunscreen are recommended when enjoying the sun and especially on a boat as the ocean are very reflective, so even those in a covered boat are exposed to rays.

Language

English and Palauan are the official language of the government and of commerce. English is commonly spoken and understood. Many elderly people are fluent in Japanese as Palau was a Japanese possession prior to WWII.

Getting There

Most visitors to Palau arrive on United Airlines daily by way of Guam, the international air service hub for the Micronesia region. From the western

Ngemelis Island

seaboard of the United States, you can hop to Hawaii, skip to Guam, then jump to Palau. Through Asia, there are twice weekly charter services between Taipei, Taiwan and Palau and additional flights are also available during peak seasons. From Europe, visitors can fly via Emerates direct to Manila, Philippines and onwards with United Airlines to Palau--this is possible without overnight stay in Manila. From main cities of departure, here is what you can expect.

To Palau from:

Guam -- 813 miles - 1 hour :45 min.
Manila -- 1041 miles - 2 hours :35 min.
Tokyo -- 2394 miles - 4 hours :25 min.
Taipei -- 2533 miles - 4 hours :55 min.
Seoul -- 2804 miles -- 5 hours : 35 min.
Los Angeles -- 7161 -- 13 hours :55 m.
New York -- 9612 -- 18 hours :55 min.

Getting Around

Taxis are plentiful and can be called to most locations, even very far away. Prices are not overly expensive and not like big cities or even Guam. Hire and rental cars, local boats and buses are also available. Hotel and dive shop transport is usually provided.

Entry & Exit

Proof of citizenship (passport or birth certificate) by U.S. citizens is required. Visas are not required. Non-U. S. citizens must have a valid passport. All visitors must have a return or onward ticket in their possession. The Chief of Immigration must approve any stay beyond 30 days.

Palau Visitor Info

Palau Visitors Authority
P.O. Box 256, Koror,
Rep. of Palau 96940
Ph: 680 488-2793
E-Mail: pva@visit-palau.com
Web: visit-palau.com

70 Islands Preserve

Departure Tax

US$20 payable on check-in before receiving boarding pass. Keep some extra cash, no credit cards accepted.
Money, Banking and Credit Cards: The U.S. dollar is the official currency. There are several U.S. FDIC insured banks operating in Palau. Most major credit cards are welcome at most visitor-oriented businesses. Cash using credit cards at the banks and at ATMs can be found in Koror. Attempts at currency exchanges are a hassle, however. Try to bring U.S. dollars. Banking hours are Mon. thru Fri. 10-3 with some islands open later on paydays or Fridays.

Time

Palau is 10 hours ahead of GMT; when it's noon Monday in Palau it is:
11:00 A.M.—Monday—in Manila
11:00 A.M.—Monday—in Taipei
Noon—Monday—in Tokyo
1:00 P.M.—Monday—in Guam
1:00 P.M.—Monday—in Sydney
5:00 P.M.—Sunday—in Honolulu
7:00 P.M.—Sunday—in Los Angeles
(PST)
10:00 P.M.—Sunday—in New York

Telecommunications/Postal

U. S. postal rates apply. The main post office is in downtown Koror and is open from 08:00 to 16:00 Mon. - Fri.; 09:00 - 10:00 Saturday, Closed Sunday and holidays. Lobby is open until 6:00P.M. daily. Palau stamps are available and considered quite collectable.
There is a communication station run by the national government and some independent telephone and computer companies in Koror. Through them, worldwide telephone, facsimile, telex, IDD, Internet/ E-Mail Service and operator-assisted dialing services are available. Phone cards are available at PNCC Office and at gas stations and stores and calls can be made from most hotels in Palau.

Ngemelis & Blue Corner

Electricity

Standard single phase 60 cycles, 110/220 volts AC U.S. type outlets are used. Adapters and converters will be needed and aren't readily available for those with 220 systems. Bring that with you.

Weights & Measures

The U.S. system of weights and measures is used. Depths are registered in feet and weights in pounds. All sale and rental dive gear is oriented this way.

What to Bring

Island style prevails. Cool, loose-fitting clothing is acceptable in most places. Hats, sunglasses and sunscreen are highly recommended. Visitors are strongly advised to respect the local customs by NOT wearing swimsuits, short-shorts or other inappropriate clothing in town, villages or public buildings. Women should wear a sarong or skirt to cover their thighs.

As far as diving gear goes, you should bring everything, but in case something breaks, there is lots of equipment for sale at the major dive shops and repair is generally available on major brands of gear, especially U.S. brands. Swimsuits are fine on the boats and on the "lunch islands."

Rental gear is also high quality and available at most dive shops. Extra weights and belts (as well as refreshments) are usually brought on every boat trip. Do not lug these along.

Underwater Photography

Palau's live aboards and the larger dive shops have fine photo pros that can shoot video or stills of your dive day or week. They can also rent still cameras and some video cameras and related gear like strobes and lenses and provide personalized training and advanced instruction. Many also offer digital labs for customers to download and edit

Underwater videographer

Ocean Hunter III meal

clean the beaches, patrol the waters, enforce environmental laws and set and maintain the moorings for the dive sites, so it is theoretically money well-spent.

Accommodations/Dining

Palau has first class hotels and a number of dependable dive operations that are constantly upgrading their services and equipment. Arrangements can also be made through local tour operators to camp in the Rock Islands.

There are hotels for every budget and desire. Arrangements can be made to stay in local homes or rustic resorts on far off islands, or at first class, every-amenity hotels right in town. The Palau Pacific Resort is currently the only facility that would be considered a dedicated dive resort in Palau. But most dive shops have package deals with

their digital files.

Underwater photo equipment sales are not common, but some items can be found. Batteries, memory cards and these kind of items are available. It is best to bring everything you need if you are serious about shooting in Palau. But if you want to try something new or just get some pictures of your adventure, it is easily done here.

Diving Permits

There are Rock Island users permits that must be purchased by all divers or visitors to the sites in Palau. These can be purchased through the dive shops and tourist agencies. These must be carried by divers and visitors while on the boats. The cost is $25 and it is valid for one month. The fees are used to

A friendly Napoleon wrasse

Going to Jellyfish Lake

some of the nicer Palau hotels that include pick-up and many hotels are very close to the dive centers. Koror isn't that large.

Tasting fine seafood cuisine in the many local restaurants is also a must. Sashimi, fish dinners and local dishes are available at a number of places in and around Koror. If you find a restaurant you like, make arrangements for some mangrove crab. You can also choose exotic local dishes as well as the ubiquitous pizza, or traditional Japanese, Chinese, Indian, Thai or American fare. There are open-air cocktail lounges, some offering live entertainment or karaoke for those not too tired from drinking in Palau's exquisite beauty.

Tipping is optional. Beer, wine and spirits are available and sold to anyone over the age of 21.

Shopping

The most sought after artform in Palau, next to the T-shirt, is undoubtedly the storyboard. These can be found at many small stores and a few of the larger ones. The Koror jail is also famous for selling the boards. Woven items, post cards and posters, books, T-shirts and some artwork can be found by perusing the various shops around Palau. A fine collection of these items can be found at the government-run Belau National Museum. There is also the Etpison private museum with a very nice variety of items and displays.

Items from endangered species are found in some shops, mostly turtle shell and black coral products like bracelets and ear rings. Divers are encouraged to discourage the creation of these products by not purchasing such items.

For food and water, the local stores all

Snorkeling Palau

sell bottled waters, soft drinks and alcoholic drinks. WCTC has a small deli and nearby the Yano Store sells local specialties.

Activities & Attractions

There are plenty of things to do in Palau besides dive. The Palau Visitor's Authority has information on all of these attractions. Ecotourism oriented activities are highly encouraged, however. The taking of shells and natural artifacts is strictly prohibited in most areas. It is advisable that the consent of the village chief be obtained before camping. Please love Palau the way you would like others to find it, beautiful and unspoiled.

- Hiking

Hiking is popular with those wanting to visit the waterfalls in Babeldaob. As tours branch out to include more than diving, new trails are being discovered and new sites mapped out as destinations. The hike to the Ngaardmau Falls takes one along a canopied jungle path, across rivers and over hills.

- Dolphin Swim

Dolphins Pacific is the large natural captive dolphin facility in the world. Bottlenose dolphins interact with visitors and snorkelers.
Contact: **www.dolphinspacific.com**

- Kayaking

Those who want a real notch in their kayak caps in Micronesia head to Palau. This huge archipelago is over 200 kilometers long and offers some of the most diverse and challenging kayaking

Palau jungle hiking

Palau Snorkeling

Snorkeling in Palau can be a rewarding experience, especially along the stunning dropoffs or at coral gardens. To best enjoy it and not damage fragile marine life, maintain neutral buoyancy to avoid knocking or brushing against marine life.

Coral is alive and easily damaged. Avoid touching, grabbing or standing on coral. It is illegal to collect corals, shells, or rather sea creatures. Be careful with your fins, as sand from fin movement can injure or smother small sea creatures. And, the undersides of rocks are home to small creatures that cannot live anywhere else. Please leave rocks, shells and coral in place for the reef dwellers who need them. Killing, damaging, riding or chasing marine life are examples of unacceptable behavior. Trash can kill marine life. Please collect any trash you see.

Rock Islands

Rock Islands

conditions in the region. Palau has tours and combined hikes for virtually every level of water enthusiast. The highlights of most of the tours are, of course, Palau's fantastic Rock Islands.

- Birding

Palau has a great variety of bird life. There are 50 species of resident birds including seabirds, land and wetland varieties. The northern atoll islands attract seabirds like frigates and noddies. The interior jungles are home to the Palauan pigeon, a tiny forest owl and kingfishers. Look for boobies, cockatoos and parrots in the Rock Islands. Palau's local conservation societies and the government's wildlife division have detailed information.

Historical Tours

Palau has a number of ancient and modern sites. Many are in the Koror area while others require a drive to Babeldaob. Those WWII buffs may want to visit the battlegrounds of Peleliu or Angaur. The Ngeremlengui area also has guns high upon a hill and remnants of the thriving agricultural era. The Stone Faces of Ollei in northern Babeldaob are a must for those who want to see the "Easter Island of Micronesia".

Diving Health Safety

Palau has two private medical clinics and a public hospital. A modern dual lock recompression chamber is available and staffed by certified operators. The Hospital Emergency number is (680) 488-2558 and the Ambulance and Fire Department number is (680) 488-1411. Police emergency number is 911. Keep well hydrated and rested to avoid decompression accidents.

Also, ensure that you have comprehensive DAN insurance and make safety decompression stops after every dive, whether you need to or not.

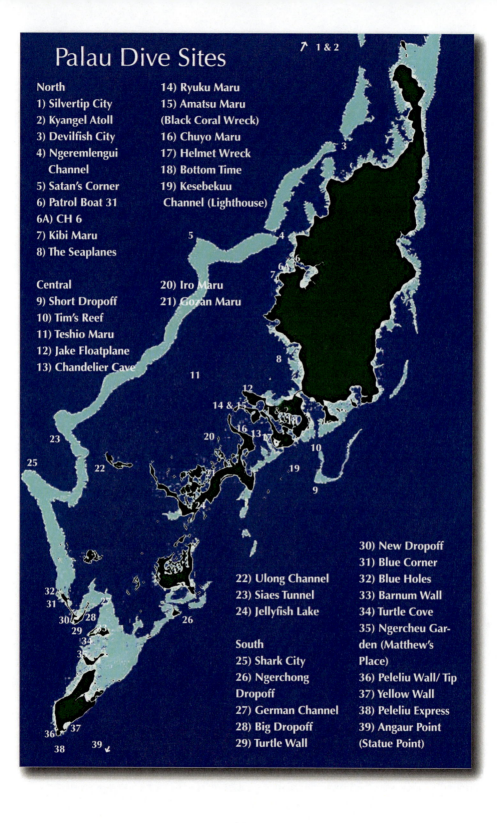

70 Islands Preserve

1) Silvertip City
Location: Far North Velasco Reef
Attractions: Big Oceanic Sharks
Depth Range: 80 to 130 feet

A good 20 miles north of Kayangel Atoll lies the north tip of Velasco Reef. The huge and shallow submerged coral reef is a treasure trove of marine life. The reef rises to 60 to 80 feet along some current swept reaches and fall into the blue.

Along the sharply sloping dropoffs, especially where coral life is thickest, are silvertip sharks in large congregations. These sharks can be found near open ocean coral reefs and are beautiful to look at with silvery bodies and strong white splotches on the tips of their dorsals and pectorals. Their swimming action and unabashed curiosity can be a little bit unnerving. They approach divers quickly, directly and often closely. As long as this happens one at a time, they seem to be no problem. They can become worrisome when they start packing up like wolves. This all adds to the excitement when dropping into the crystal blue to look for congregations of silvertips and other carcharias family members.

A dive here is always a current ride, rolling along the eastern slope with sapphire triggerfish called blue tangs dotting the reef, vase and porites corals in lone formations, sea whips and some fans along the slopes and silvertips coming in from the blue. Grey reef sharks are also sometimes present. Rainbow runners also like this terrain. The silvertips vary in size from 2 feet to 10 feet, averaging 4 feet on the reeftop but larger the deeper over the edge one ventures. There is also a good chance of seeing other sharks here like bronze

Giant gorgonian fans

whalers, oceanic whitetips and even tiger sharks. Blue marlin and sailfish may also be seen occasionally. The chance of seeing pelagics like wahoo are also good here as well as king mackerel. Large dolphin schools and even sperm whales also roam here.

There is a series of reefs along the top of Velasco with deep water sea grasses also intermixed that are home to small invertebrates. Look here for large, healthy stands of cabbage coral and beautiful hard vase corals on the broad reeftop.

At the southern end of Velasco is **Ngeurangel Reef**, which has coral and a sand spit that break the surface. There are five shipwrecks found here, but they are broken up or have been salvaged.

One of the most notable is the **Samidare**. This Japanese fleet destroyer was found and identified by the late wreck hunter Klaus Lindemann and Francis Toribiong with Kyangel chief Radochol Rulukel in 1990.

The ship, which had grounded in August 1944 and was later sunk. It has been totally salvaged with the exception of some massive parts. There are two large propeller shafts, parts of the turbine housing, some gun barrels, a fire extinguisher, a machine gun, some plating and some shells next to a large chain.

Kyangel dolphins

The wreck known as the **George Bush Wreck** also is found here. Discovered by Dan Bailey, it, too, is broken and salvaged. This is the ship former U.S. President George Bush is supposed to have sunk when he was a young WWII Navy fighter pilot.

The surrounding reef is that of a surf zone, not too abundant with major growth, but deeper water produces some nice hard corals and scattered anemones along with some curious grey reef sharks that want to know what's up. Divers probably only come here a couple of times a year at most.

2) Kyangel Atoll
Location: Outer Reef, Kyangel
Attractions: Corals, Dropoff
Depth Range: 25 to 130 feet

One of the most beautiful atolls in the world and one of the most photographed in that of Kyangel in northern Palau. It is the quintessential

Pacific atoll, with a school of spinner dolphins living at the entrance channel mouth. The inner lagoon is varying shades of emerald, turquoise and azures. One main island and three smaller ones all have idyllic beaches, small stands of corals on a sandy bottom and lush growths of palms and jungle. Less than 100 people live on the main island and the others are uninhabited. Frigates, noddies, boobies, Pacific whitebirds and terns all live on the beach-lined isles or come to the islands at night to roost or hover. At night, the Milky Way and lolling waves on a Kayangel island create the ideal atmosphere to spend an evening before taking off for Velasco and other adventures.

The diving on the reefs around Kyangel can be quite good, with pelagic action, large schools of fish and beautiful formations of corals and outcrops. At **Virgin Sacrifice**, located just south of Kyangel in the passage between the reef and the atoll, a long and pleasant dive can be made drifting with the current. A shelf running from 40-50 feet on the north to as shallow as 25 feet on the west tops off the upper reef. A nice dropoff with whip corals and some gorgonian sea fans accents the current swept sloping drop.

Be careful to watch what the current is doing as it can take the diver off the wall and out to open sea, effectively aborting the dive plan. The upper reef is very beautiful with schools of brilliant yellowstripe sweetlips, black snapper and yellow-spot emperors being among the schooling fish found at the various large coral heads.

This manta may have lost a mandible in a fishing net. It got healed at the cleaning station at Devilfish City

The upper reef current sweeps along reeftop for an easy drift dive over stands of table corals and platter corals. Also look for nudibranchs and other nice invertebrate life here.

On the outer reef to the east, Kyangel also has a **Blue Hole** that starts rather deep at around 80 feet and runs down through a chasm open along a wall at a healthy 160 feet.

The **Kyangel Wall** can also bring many thrills with drift diving and the promise of pelagic life. Silvertip sharks and grey reef sharks can be seen there and other big fish are common. The area is also known as a haven for golden cowries. The outer reef is not diveable much of the year, so if a diver gets to the outer barrier reef on a clam day, cherish the moment and enjoy the dive.

3) Devilfish City
Location: Ngaardmau Channel
Attractions: Mantas, Soft Coral
Depth Range: 30 to 80 feet

This site along the western coast of northern Babeldaob combines channel diving with some visits to some nearby soft coral-covered cleaning stations that are often frequented by reef and ocean-going manta rays. The channel is like most that lead from mangroves to the sea in that visibility

Mantas at the channel

As the current increases, look for more feeding and sometimes mating activity. In recents years, there has been a shift away from the cleaning stations but mantas are still frequently seen feeding in the channle mouth. They are also seen moving up and down the channel.

shifts with the incoming incoming and outgoing tides. A high, slack tide will see the least current, best visibility. The rays don't like to work too much when cleaning, but they do like some current.

The sides of the channel are lined with massive fields of sea whips, soft corals, sea fans and large stands of evergreen tubastrea corals. The depth here is around 80 feet. The fish that get active as the current picks up include rainbow runners, reef sharks, bumphead parrotfish and fusiliers.

Off the channel is a set of sea fan adorned coral heads in a flats area above the channel. At the far coral head in about 45 feet of water, the mantas come in to clean. The diver can see this station easily as there

Manta at Devilfish City

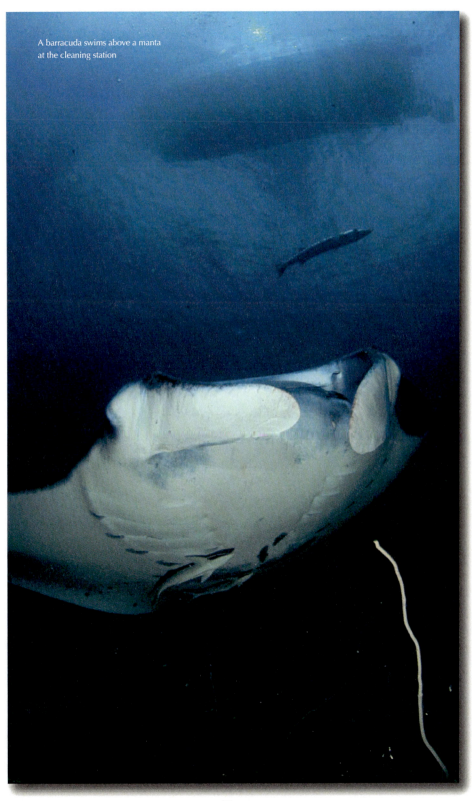

A barracuda swims above a manta at the cleaning station

Ngeremlengui Channel soft corals

are hundreds of copper sweeper baitfish in the coral head and it is adorned with both gorgonians and soft corals. Evene with no mantas, this station is pretty for photos and worth a visit.

Here, butterflyfish and wrasses wait for the mantas to come in. On a good day, the mantas will be lined up almost like jets at a major airport. They will wait their turn to get to the cleaners and then hover. Mantas don't like to be touched or chased, so find an unobtrusive place near the cleaning site and wait quietly and remain as motionless as possible. The mantas will come quite close and the cleaning behavior will continue for some time.

A drift out the channel will also bring some surprises like striped skipjack schools and at one point two shocking pink anemones with an electric blue tridacna clam next to them.

4) Ngeremlengui Channel or West Passage
Location: West-Central Babeldaob
Attractions: Lively Channel
Depth Range: 20 to 110 feet

This pass is located about one-third of the way up the western coast of Babeldaob, which is Palau's largest and highest island. The pass, also known as West Passage, is near an area where two large rivers empty into the ocean. The rich nutrients from the river feed the expansive mangroves that are the center of juvenile marine growth. The result of this mangrove hatchery is a great variety of marine animals that inhabit the nearby channel.

The nutrients also feed the corals and create large growths of sea fans, tall stands of evergreen cup corals and brilliant soft corals that grow in a variety of hues. The mangroves are also the main home of Palau's crocodiles.

The current runs swiftly here most of the time. This should be regarded as a drift dive and the diver should have safety sausage (actually on every Palau dive).

The wall along the pass ranges from a sharp slope to totally vertical most of the time. There are even places that are undercut, providing overhangs that have sea fans and black coral trees. While these walls are current swept and not as thick in growth as places like Ngemelis (Big Dropoff), they have a good variety of invertebrate life, sea whips, crinoids, anemones and all of those critters that like to filter feed in currents.

There are sites along the wall, especially between the two red channel markers, that have sandy slopes. Many kinds of fusiliers like these walls as do huge schools of striped snappers. Brilliant yellowtails and electric blues course by at the outcroppings, providing a show of motion and color. Larger sharks, Napoleon wrasses and dogtooth tuna also swim by in the blue or below on the channel floor.

The grey reef sharks can be very territorial here and not as laid back as those along the Blue Corner. If they start giving a territorial display, get out of their territory by slowly ascending to a shallower depth.

This has been one of the few places a mesekiu, or Palauan dugong, has been photographed underwater. These sea cows are similar to Florida manatees but have been hunted in the past and

Palauan Dugong at Ngeremlengui

have adapted to open ocean for resting during the day to avoid predation. At night they come into the shallows to munch on sea grasses. The one photographed (P.33) had at least six remoras attached to its back and they were flapping like flags in the breeze. It had a school of yellow-stripe pilotfish at its nose swimming like mad.

If one is lucky, a school of spinner dolphins may appear and give a show, leaping from the sea with acrobatic moves. It can be a beautiful sight as the animals frolic, framed in the background by the majestic hillside jungles of Babeldaob.

5) Satan's Corner
Location: West-Central Babeldaob
Attractions: Schooling Fish & Pelagics
Depth Range: 20 to 80 feet

Palau crocodile

The beauty of diving in Palau is that just when you think you may have possibly seen it all, someone comes along and discovers a whole new undersea experience for you to enjoy, be amazed at and be thrilled by.

The western slopes of Ngeremlengui outer reef offer just the ticket. This broad pass is fed by a twin river system that empties into Karamadoo Bay. The bay then empties via a snaking channel into the southern Philippine Sea. The outer reefs just south of this pass are rarely dived and offer surprises at every turn. The incredible nutrients flushed into the sea feed spectacular coral growth on the upper reef slopes. Deeper, yawning slopes, current-swept flats and deep undersea points and dropoffs provide a varied terrain that attracts some awesome marine life.

Getting there requires a calm day and a high tide doesn't hurt. The reason it should be calm is that some of the best spots are found outside the pass and a little south along a jutting point in the reef.

On those special days when the sea is calm and the sky is blue and windless, hop in. Don't expect the sharp dropoffs of the south or even the extremely clear water. But at the Sata's Corner do expect rich coral gardens and surprises that can come in from the depths. Eagle rays are known to like this place a lot. The spotted eagle ray and the even rarer ornate eagle ray are seen here often. The ornate eagle ray has an extremely long tail as an adult, looking like a living kite and it sails

through the water.

In the shallower areas, look for a host of varied sea anemones and a variance of clownfish as well. They sit on top of large coral heads surrounded by clouds of fairy salmon and hot pink basslets and electric blue chromis.

6) Patrol Boat 31
Location: Ngeremeduu Bay
Attractions: WWII Japanese Destroyer
Depth Range: 0 to 90 feet

The ship is the converted Momi Class destroyer Kiku. It lies in a river channel (complete with possible saltwater crocs) in central Babelthuap. It may not be a dive for everyone as there can be tricky currents, low visibility, green water and a lot of wreckage, but for the adventurous this dive is worth it.

The wreck starts on the shoreline at Karamanadoo Bay where shore hugging clams and mussels heavily encrust the shoreline and poke above the surface at low tide. Parts of the ship appear in two feet of water and cascade down to the bottom that flattens out at around 70 feet and eventually drops deeper.

This wreck is broken but is still intact enough to probe. There is heavy silt, so care must be taken, but the openings provide areas to explore and river snappers, batfish and groupers use this wreck as a haven. The ship still has its coral-covered stern gun, which sits pointing downward. The 14cm shells sit on the sea floor nearby in what is left of the seaworm-eaten wooden boxes that once held them. Nearby are sea pens.

There is a lot to see at around ten feet if a safety decompression is in order. There is still some wreckage and parts of the boiler and engine room are prominent.

Try to dive this wreck at slack, high tide as the visibility should probably be best, about 25 feet, at this time.

The river silt is fine but there is good coral growth on parts of the Kiku wreck.

Overgrown in tubastreas, the PB 31's gun is a sea life haven now.

Lionfish and baitfish hover over the Kiku.

Bowgun of CH 26 and black coral

Channel super large sea fan

6A) Patrol Boat CH 26
Location: Ngeremlengui Channel
Attractions: WWII Sub Chaser
Depth Range: 130 to 140+ feet

This deep ship just found in mid-2015, 72 years after its demise, lies on its port side and boasts nice growths of black coral, quite a bit of damage midships and enjoys some fish life. Its final resting place is in a deep and sandy channel at the bottom of a fairly steep, sea fan adorned wall.

This new wreck is a special class of sub chaser called the CH Number 26. As it is deep on the border of sport diving limits, bottom time for scuba is short. The bowgun is intact, covered with coral and the gun still on its base. The ship itself lays on the port side. Midships has severe damage around the bridge area. This is probably where it was struck and sunk. The remains of the aft sit farther back in this sandy but deep channel.

The ship's captain was 37-year-old Eiji Kato. He and three other officers died in the attack and 11 others (total crew of 15) were injured. The captain left behind a wife and four children.

The wall has some huge gorgonian fans and nice hard corals up shallow.

Bridge area damage

KB Bridge

7) Kibi Maru
Location: Inner Channel
Attractions: Overturned WWII wreck
Depth Range: 20 to 90 feet

This large freighter can be a very good dive for those wanting to see encrusting marine life in many forms. For the shipwreck buff, this is also an odd log entry as the ship sits upside down but can be explored. The main hinderance here is the currents. The ship originally was strafed and then nearly bombed in the WWII action that brought it to its demise. It was beached on a reef on the inner passage that leads to the main exit to West Passage. It was salvaged there after the war and later slid down into deeper water where it came to rest upside-down in 90 feet of water.

Try to time this dive when the tide is high and slack to get the best visibility and the least current. The upper reef here is nice with lots of acropora and small reef tropicals. The dive down the steep slope reveals large branching evergreen tubastreas and some pieces from the ship. Some of this wreckage has nice soft coral trees growing on it. Look also for large groupers.

The entire side of the ship is covered in a mass of encrusting corals, sponges, fans, sea whips and other invertebrate life that can be good, albeit challenging with the currents, for close-up photography. The bow is bent and buckled somewhat and is a true forest of sea whips. Look for other marine creatures in the bow forest like pipefish, razor clams and starfish. Look for shrimp and gobies on the whips themselves. The inner sanctum of the ship can be visited by going to the starboard side away from the western channel wall and entering in the open spaces that lead to the dark and wide open holds. It is not advised to try to squeeze into bridge areas, poop, etc. as they are undoubtedly unstable.

This space will also allow you to avoid current. The sea floor and inside

Seaplane prop

of the ship has some interesting growth of antipathes corals (black corals). There are also golden sea fans and some large soft corals at the aft of the Kibi. Wreck divers and invertebrate hunters will certainly like this ship and location, although the average diver may not be as thrilled.

8) The Seaplanes
Location: Southern Babelthuap, Palau
Attractions: Jake-Aichi Floatplanes
Depth Range: 0 to 20 feet

The remnants of the Jake-Aichi floatplanes barely sit beneath the water on the Babeldaob side of the KB Bridge. Nestled in some Rock Islands, one is in fairly good condition, while the other has been exposed to waves and is pretty well broken up. Aichi built the Jake in 1938, meaning these planes were virtually brand new when the war started. They had two principle roles. The first a crew of three and a cargo of bombs but was rather slow in this role. The other was as a long-range reconnaissance plane. This suited the plane much better. They could also berth easily in lagoons. One of the Jakes sits near the cave where the last crocodile to kill a man in Palau was hunted down. The plane is scattered but the prop and engine are visible and can be easily snorkeled.

By far the best Jake specimen is nestled across from the cave. The wings with little coral growth stretch out broadly. The engine has fallen forward, probably from its own weight, but the pilot's seat is still intact. The floats of the plane can be seen here as well, with one still in place under a wing. The metal of a sunken plane can be jagged, so take care when exploring these sites. It is best to come here at high tide.

Chambered nautilus

CENTRAL PALAU

9) Short Dropoff
Location: East-Central Outer Reef
Attractions: Dropoff, Batfish Schools
Depth Range: 20 to 130 feet

Short Dropoff got its name mainly because it is but a short boat ride from Koror. Located near a cut in the outer barrier reef on the archipelago's east side, Short Dropoff provides a great variety of sea life, especially for the macro critter photographer.

Once at the dive site, a quick snorkel will reveal an upper reef flat crowded with corals and tons of reef tropicals. This garden gradually slopes down to about 35 feet and then drops off abruptly. In some spots it is a sheer wall but in other places it is a sandy fall. The diving here is usually done on the protected inner reef wall. The depth can be whatever the diver wants, with sponges and branching corals at the 40 to 50 foot mark, making it quite safe for a long, exploratory dive. Look especially for crocodilefish sitting in ambush in the corals and sand. It is likely that divers will encounter hawksbill turtles resting on the ledges or munching on some hydroids. Throughout the dive, schools of yellowtail fusiliers will appear from above and below and swim by curiously. Short Drop also has good reef shark action at the point as well as schooling batfish. Short Drop is also a good place for chambered nautilus photography as well.

10) Tim's Reef
Location: Near Mutremdiu, Palau
Attraction: Sunken Zeke Fighter
Depth Range: 5 to 70 feet

Very few people dive here, but I think it is a marvelous place to dive and snorkel. When we first found the spot, I told my pal Francis Toribiong that I liked the place and he said let's call it "Tim's Reef". Since then, the '98 El Nino killed all of the absolutely amazing table coral formations at reeftop, but it still has great coral down below and has WWII history as well.

It is located about half the way out to Short Dropoff and features a somewhat circular reef surrounded by a couple of channels that are full of life. The best location is on the southwest side. Divers can go down the slope to staghorn coral flats that have lots of chromis. In about 60 feet there is a very intact, upside down Japanese Zeke fighter. The guns and wings are still in place. A look underneath to the cockpit will reveal small glassy sweepers in a large school. Look for leaf fish in the engine compartment area.

This site combines history with a beautiful reef. Eagle rays have been seen in schools here swimming in the current. You can swim around the whole reef and dive all around Tim's to find new surprises.

11) Teshio Maru
Location: 5 miles NE Palau Pacific
Attractions: Holds, corals, barracuda
Typical Depth Range: 45 to 90 feet

This ship sunk while underway apparently trying to get out of Palau by heading north to the main channel. It now rests on its starboard side. It is subject to swells as the port side is only about 45 feet from the surface and is shaken pretty good after big storms. Despite this fact, the coral growth is very nice around the ship's bridge and on the port side, with intricate platter corals sprawling broadly and small juvenile fish inhabiting the protecting cover of the lacey formations. It is one of the fishiest wrecks in Palau,

Teshio bowgun

Jake Floatplane

with blackbar barracuda schools coming in and also striped skipjack shoals. The water here is much clearer than at most of Palau's shipwrecks and the entire wreck can be seen from the surface on snorkel on a particularly good day. Also, look for various grouper species that live in the acropora corals. The mast has a lot of blue chromis busily flitting about and anemones are found at various intervals. On occasion a very large, solitary barracuda is also seen near the ship.

The engine room was blasted by salvagers but is open. It is still wise to stay out of it, as the whole area is unstable. There is damage at the fore and aft of the ship. These hits apparently caused it to sink.

12) Jake Floatplane
Location: North of Meyuns Ramp
Attractions: Upright WWII Floatplane
Depth Range: 35 to 50 feet

This floatplane, an Aichi E13A or Jake type reconnaissance seaplane, is one of the most intact plane wrecks in Micronesia. It sits mostly upright with wings and one float still intact in shallow water not too far off the Meyuns seaplane ramp. There is also another plane wreck closer to the ramp, a Jake or possibly a Rufe, but it's cloth body covering has disintegrated and it is heavily overgrown with coral.

The plane sits surrounded by a coral garden and one float is nearby and coral encrusted. The plane itself still

Jake Floatplane

Chandelier Cave

has some of its window glass in place. Nice coral growth is found along one wing and small sea whips and other encrusting marine growth is found all over the plane. The wreck has a resident batfish that will pose for photographers It lives beneath the fuselage.

The marine life in the area is good for macrophotography as well. Look for whitecap shrimp in the razor corals and colorful juvenile tropical fish in the coral heads.

13) Chandelier Cave
Location: Rock Islands near Koror
Attractions: Freshwater caves
Depth Range: 10 to 35 feet

Chandelier Cave is a real departure from reef diving. Located in the Rock Islands near Sam's Tours, this shallow cave comprises many chambers and a high ceiling that rises above the water level, allowing divers to surface, talk and even take off diving gear and walk around in some of the chambers. The entry is made at a small cove in the Rock Islands at about 20 to 25 feet through a jungle undercut. Take special care to stay up and away from the ocean floor. It is silt covered and stirs up easily. The light at the entrance is your exit reference, so it is especially wise to keep the water clear.

It is pitch black inside this cave without a light. There are stalactites and stalagmites to abruptly halt your progress, so don't even attempt to swim in without a dependable light. Once inside, it is a limestone fantasyland with an upper layer of fresh water that is crystal clear. The cave formations can be seen easily and a short swim will bring the diver to the first chamber. Here, huge dripstones hang from the chamber's ceiling.

The beauty of the inner cave combined with the water clarity gives the impression of unending visibility. A diver can get out of the water here and explore a small tunnel if the spirit moves him or her. In all, there are four chambers that lead back to a large area where divers can again doff gear, get out of the water and walk around. The beauty of the dripstone and the chandelierlike forms make this a favorite novelty dive for many. The reef in front is also worth exploring as there are some unusual corals and fish here including mandarinfish, dragonets and colorful gobies.

14) Ryuko Maru
Location: Near Palau Pacific Resort
Attractions: Upright WWII Shipwreck
Depth Range: 60 to 110 feet

This interesting wreck lies just a stone's throw south of the Palau Pacific Resort along the northwestern shore of Ngargol Island. Covered in black coral trees and full of marine life like skipjacks and lionfish, the ship is a pleasant overswim and there are parts that can be easily penetrated. There are some brilliant golden gorgonians on the hold edges.

The bow sits in about 70 feet of water with the deck dipping to 90 and it is 120 feet inside the holds. The holds are mostly empty as they were either salvaged or without cargo when it was hit. A portion of the stand of what appears to be the ship's compass is still on the first level of the bridge. The ship burned heavily before sinking in the midships area, so there is little in the way of wood left. There is also a machine gun buried in the heavy silt in the bridge.

A nice feature of the ship is the outer passageway that runs along both sides of the lower bridge and accesses the various quarters and the engine room catwalk. The adoring wire corals and black corals are full of tiny baitfish during certain times of the year. Look also for various kinds pipefish that like the wreck habitats as homes.

The engine room is open and accessible as it was blasted by salvagers so the boilers could be removed. Bombs are found nearby in shallower water. Some of the damages, especially those found around the bridge area, are from a direct hit of an aerial bomb during the Desecrate air raid of March 1944. .

15) Amatsu Maru
Location: Ngederrak lagoon
Attractions: Large Japanese tanker
Depth Range: 70 to 130 feet

The Amatsu Maru is one of the newer ships sitting on the ocean floor in Palau. It was built during the war and sunk during the Desecrate 1 carrier raid of March 30-31, 1944. It is one of the best wreck dives. It is close to Koror, located on the southern side of Ngerchol Island in Ngederrak lagoon. It is heavily covered with corals, is a haven for fish and still retains many of its wartime features.

This ship is often called the Black Coral Wreck and rightly so. The trees of this golden, wispy, golden coral heavily adorn this ship. They are so thick that in some places they make it difficult to enter passages. Lionfish prey on glassfish that live in the black coral.

They make good photo subjects nestled in the black coral trees. This ship is about 500 yards long and deeper than most of the Palau shipwrecks. The deck depth averages between 90 and 110 feet and the visibility is not always the greatest, so some planning and thought is essential when exploring this ship.

This ship was a tanker and it has a split superstructure, catwalks covering piping and a pumphouse. Look for unusual and thick invertebrate sea life on these walks, which is somewhat reminiscent of Chuuk's Shinkoku Maru. There are many places fore to poke around and explore. The forecastle can be entered easily and is spacious but can still be silty. A light is necessary while exploring.

The bridge has a large rail atop it that is heavily covered with black coral, as are some of the passageways. The passageways are passable but don't be surprised if you get tangled in some kind of coral. This ship is in an area that is normally protected and free of currents.

16) Chuyo Maru
Location: Near Malakal Anchorage
Attractions: WWII wreck with heavy coral growth, fish
Depth Range: 30 to 120 feet

This ship is still in fine shape and is laden in coral and a home for fish. The bridge is in 70 feet of water and it is 90 feet to the deck. The top of the mast, the crosstree, is a garden of coral, sponges and fishes. There is a resident school of sharpnose barracuda that especially like the bridge aft areas. The intact masts also attract various schools of fusiliers. Cock's comb oysters are thick on this wreck. The forward mast is especially nice.

The bow is full of sea life and there can be a current running off the bow making it also a good place to look for schooling fish. The anchor chain stretches down sharply into the sand. Farther back, forward of the bridge on the port side, a large anchor also sits on the deck. The bridge can be on several levels. It is very silty, so take photos quickly before it gets too stirred up. Even if one goes very slowly and uses extremely neutral buoyancy to keep conditions favorable, one's air bubbles may cause a rain of silt.

The navigation area of the bridge has a fallen

Batfish on the upper deck

Helmet wreck artifacts

but still intact ship's telegraph.

The discovery of this wreck came when the Francis and Klaus Lindemann had been looking, searching, identifying and exploring and were at the end of their week and the end of their safe diving time. Lindemann was scheduled to fly out the next day and decided to let accumulated nitrogen purge itself from his system.

So when they took a morning spin to the old anchorage site near Koror to check out the bottom with the finder, it was Toribiong who elected to dive down to check out an echo that looked like a large wreck on the screen. The trouble was, as far as Toribiong could recall, no one locally had fished there, so the possibility of there being a wreck so close to a major population center was pretty remote.

"I dived down and down and was almost at the bottom and still there was no ship," recalls Toribiong.

Resigning the sighting to some sort of phantom, he decided to ascend. "I picked up the anchor line and turned around and there it was."

17) Helmet Wreck
Location: Malakal Harbor
Attractions: Munitions, war artifacts
Depth Range: 28 to 95 feet

This ship has been given a number of monikers, including Helmet Wreck, Mystery Wreck and Depth Charge Wreck. Experts are still trying to identify it properly as it was obviously being used by the Japanese for the war effort, but does not appear to be Japanese built. It was a fairly recent discovery by wreck expert Dan Bailey and is a treasure trove of war materials.

It is known as the Helmet Wreck for its cargo of helmets that are now fused together from being in the ocean for nearly six decades. It sits on a sloping bank with the stern in 50 feet of water and the bow in about 100 feet. It is a new ship, as an inspection of its engine room shows a triple expansion, single shaft steam engine. Oddly, an inspection of the ship's coal bin (used to

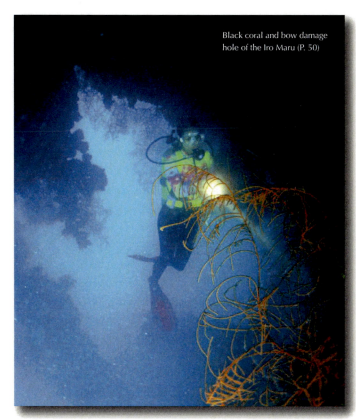

Black coral and bow damage hole of the Iro Maru (P. 50)

fuel the engines and cook stove) shows little coal. It may not have been in use at the time it went down.

The ship has three holds, one in the stern and two in the bow area, with the ship's superstructure and engine room in between. The rear hold displays massive damage, the obvious result of a powerful explosion. The starboard deck plating and side plating was blown completely back, curling until it almost touches the intact sides and deck of the bow. The bowgun apparently was jarred from its mount by the explosion and lays on its side. The companion ladder and platform ladder were also doubled over and the mast ladder has fallen onto the gun platform. The mast crosstree is missing. The top of the bow mast extends to within 28 feet of the surface and is overgrown with corals and encrusting marine life.

The forward section of the hold is packed with round canisters about the size of thirty-gallon drums. These are depth charges... thus the name depth charge wreck. This hold also contains encrusted carbine rifles, ammunition, stacks of helmets and gas masks. The bridge floorboards have disappeared but the helm and the brass ring of the wheel (marine worms eat the wood, leaving only the brass) are present and laying on their sides. Some artifacts have been stolen by selfish souvenir seekers. But when found, the galley had pots, pans, bottles, cups, dishes, claret glasses, a coal burning stove and other utensils. There is also a small radio room with equipment still in place. The engine room has been protected from heavy silting. Other sea life that heavily encrusts the ship along with the black coral includes clams, jagged oysters, and sponges. The ship's stack is missing and sits on the reef along the starboard side of the ship. These usually weaken with the years on WWII wrecks.

The forward holds contain assorted electrical parts and fixtures. It is possible to swim from the center hold to the forward hold, as the partition 'tween decks is gone. The most notable pieces of cargo are three large airplane engines in the forward hold.

The boson's locker in the bow contains some beautiful storm lanterns and a taff rail log any seasoned navigator would love to have a look at. The lightbulb in the locker is still intact in the overhead light fixture. The outside of the ship is covered in encrusting coral and invertebrate life, with the stern area being especially interesting.

Along the starboard, Francis Toribiong found a small bugle in the silt on the ocean floor. An odd and unique piece of memorabilia. This ship is just minutes away from most Koror dive shops and is full of so much it may take a couple of dives to fully appreciate.

18) Bottom Time Bar & Grill Corner
Location: Sam's Tours
Attractions: Unusual Life, Muck Dive
Depth Range: 0 to 20 feet

This area around the Bottom Time Bar & Grill at Sam's Tours Dive Shop may jokingly be dubbed "Brown Corner" in reference to its stark contrast to the famous Blue Corner. But it is a popular muck diver's site and a haven for mandarinfish, banded pipefish and

Mating mandarinfish

other tiny critters. The entire dive can be done in less than six feet of water by just poking along the wall and seeing what lives in and around it. Above you, the guests at Sam's down Red Rooster beers and munch immense burgers as the sun sets off the Pincers channel mouth. The mandarinfish come out at dusk, so bring a light if the goal is to see them.

This site also holds many more macro surprises aside from the mandarins. A variety of small crabs and shrimp live in the rocks. The silty slope nearby has a clams and a resident banded sea snake and some very coy and camouflaged cuttlefish. The outer reef near the channel is the home of parrotfish, a school of jacks, a school of batfish and crocodile needlefish.

This is best dived when the tide is high. At low tide, the waves action from boats going by causes the silt to stir up and reduces visibility and causes scatter in photos. Boats do come and go here so keep clear of the docking areas. But there is a lot to see in a small area so just take it slow and be watchful for tiny invertebrates and odd fish.

Macro is the norm here as other tiny creatures seen here include the banded fantail pipefish, cardinalfish, frogfish and spotted goby. Other good muck dives in and around Koror include the dock in front of NECO Marine, the Malakal dock when it is not busy, the Marina Hotel's dock and pier and the coral rubble in front of Chandelier Cave, where mandarins also stay.

19) Kesebukuu Channel (Lighthouse)
Location: Malakal Pass
Attractions: Ship, coral thickets
Depth Range: 20 to 80 feet

There is a ship located in the channel near one of the channel markers and is referred to locally as the Channel Marker Wreck. It apparently was a Japanese fishing ship configured into a sub chaser as it has large holds with coils that were used to refrigerate the catch. The gun from the small gun platform on the bow has been removed. Today it sits at the bottom of a slope in a place with a swift current. When descending the slope you will see incredible stands of green tube corals. At night, the green tube coral polyps extend and are magnificent photo subjects. Take care with these as they can be jagged. The ship sits at the bottom of the sandy channel at a slight list and looms out of the blue. It is large enough that if the current is a problem the diver can duck behind the appropriate side of the ship and be perfectly sheltered.

The deck is covered with ever-increasing growths of soft corals and sea fans. Flurries of brightly colored tropical fish feed madly in the current that passes over the top of the ship. The action is great and the upper bridge

Fusiliers on the wreck

Jack school on Iro

feel like fighting the current to see the ship (the current varies front weak to ripping, so check the tide changes), a shallow dive on the upper part of the channel on a sunny day is a marvelous experience. It is also considered a great night dive with colorful crinoids and accompanying clingfish and squat lobsters, basket stars, many varieties of nudibranchs.

At the end of the channel is a lighthouse and manta rays have been seen congregating here.

20) Iro Maru
Location: Urukthapel Bay
Attractions: Large, upright WWII oiler
Depth: 50 to 120 feet

is small but easily explored. There are some immense angelfish around this wreck. The rudder has disintegrated, but there are still three supports that stick out the back of the ship. The propeller has been removed.

The shallow reef up the channel wall is an incredible dive all by itself. Cuttlefish huddle over carpets of staghorn coral. Silver and blue chromis and golden anthias live in these immense spreads of staghorn coral and feed with wild abandon, giving this reef a kaleidoscopic effect. There are numerous table and platter corals and some large sea anemones. If you don't

The Iro is perhaps the best-known and most popular shipwreck in Palau. It is located just a short distance from Koror and is in an area that is normally protected from winds and rough seas. It is basically shallow as wrecks go and is beautifully overgrown with many forms of sessile marine life. Its sister ship, the Sata lies close by, upside-down, deep and basically undivable.

This ship was an oiler and a small oil slick can still be seen in the area. The first thing the diver notes upon descent is the schooling bigeye jacks around

Iro bowgun

the masts. The crossmembers are heavily encrusted with hard corals and oysters. On rare occasions, the shellfish can be seen spawning and the fusiliers will gather around for a free meal. Divers are also likely to be greeted by a resident school of batfish that aren't at all shy. The Iro was built in 1922. She was sunk in March of 1944 and was also the subject of some salvage after the war. Many of the ships in Palau were salvaged in some way and this is why places like the bridge areas are usually stripped here.

The Iro was the victim of a submarine torpedo attack prior the Desecrate One air raid and her bow displays a large crescent where a hit took place. This is not the damage that caused her to sink, although the hole is well-defined it may appear so. A diver can actually swim through this hole, which is now heavily overgrown with black coral and sponges. The thick anchor chain runs nearby.

The bow gun is mounted on a huge platform. This, too, is overgrown with delicate, wispy black coral trees and shell, fish and invertebrate life. It is an older gun with a caliber of 14 centimeters and a low trajectory.

The aft ship has a number of overgrown pipes, derricks and a beautiful mast configuration. The galley is also located back here but is pretty thick in silt and should be explored only by the prepared and experienced. Pots, pans and a stove are recognizable. It is in the tall deckhouse located in front of the poop deck. The aft also holds a large gun. The ship can be seen in one dive, but two are better.

Swimming with bottlenose dolphins at Dolphins Pacific

21) Gozan Maru
Location: Rock Islands
Attractions: Shipwreck, Reeflike corals
Depth Range: 25 to 80 feet

The Gozan Maru was discovered by Francis Toribiong while making an aerial search of the Rock Islands for dive sites and unique formations. It was found in 1984 and is very much intact. It went down on its side and now lists heavily to port. It has not been positively identified and may be a ship other than the Gozan. The shallow part of the hull closest to the surface resembles a reef. All types of corals have latched on to this wreck, from brain, platter and star corals to large leather corals. Sea anemones are interspersed with this growth and come with a variety of clownfish. One purple-tipped anemone with skunk clownfish is especially photogenic. A tridacna sits nearby. Small schools of a half-dozen barracuda roam this ship and at times approach close enough to be photographed.

The foremast has become a haven for all sorts of marine invertebrates. Tridacna clams nestle between corals

Rock Island sunset

and one-stripe clownfish are thick in large colonies of bubble anemones. Clams, oysters, whip corals and bulb corals are all heavily congregated on the shallow mast. Schooling fish are thick, especially small basslets that make for colorful subjects for photography.

Swimming through the ship itself can be a little disorienting as it lists heavily to port. The deck is overgrown only by an occasional razor or Faulkner mushroom anemone coral. The holds are empty, but the second hold shows the damage that put the ship down. Klaus Lindemann surmises it was caused by a 1000 lb. bomb. The explosion apparently tore the bottom plates loose and the result is a jagged, inwardly bent, gaping hole large enough for a diver to easily swim through. Some water flows through here as a large sea fan and other gorgonians, soft corals and stinging hydroids have taken root. This ship is generally free of any noticeable current, however. The upper bridge and rear are quite worthy of exploration. Stay out of the engine room. It is extremely dark, rife with pipes and loose wires and disorienting from the list. A person can get into real trouble in there.

The aft has a fallen mast and small deck gun to observe. There is a ship nearby that is completely blown apart and the shock wave from this ship's massive explosion may explain some of the damage done to the Gozan. The nearby ship is the **Kamikaze Maru** and it is really torn apart. There are some explosives on the Kamikaze still in what remains of the forward holds. This ship is best left alone. Instead, spend a couple of dives on the Gozan, it is worthy of the extra exploration and photography.

22) Ulong Channel
Location: West of Ulong Island
Attractions: Lettuce corals, drift dive
Depth Range: 20 to 80 feet

This pass near Ulong Island provides one great ride past underwater terrain that appears to be landscaped. Ulong Island is the kind of tropical paradise a person would like to come upon if shipwrecked. It has beautiful sandy beaches, tall coconut trees and rich, green vegetation. Large cliffs loom up, protecting the flora and birds soar through the skies.

Cabbage corals

Coral stand in Ulong Channel

In fact, it was where Captain James Wilson wrecked the Antelope and accidentally discovered Palau for the Western world. There is a plaque to that effect on the island's beach.

Underwater nearby Ngerumekaol Pass is one of the best drift dives Palau has to offer. Dotted with huge coral heads and steep slopes on each side, the soft and fan coral cover appears to have been placed by a landscaping expert. Brilliant crinoids and jet-black ones sit out in the daytime to filter feed. Big and occasionally exotic fish, like the spectacular threadfin pompano that usually inhabit open ocean, frequent this spillway. It is the spawning grounds for large groupers and a popular resting-place for hawksbill turtles. The groupers are protected from fishing by law and have actually been seen schooling here, a very rare phenomenon.

Whitetip and grey reef sharks are commonly seen especially at the mouth of the channel. Even a tiger shark has been reported. The action here is excellent during the changing of the tides. More than one diver has had a pesky remora leave a shark or turtle and try to attach itself during a channel dive. One of the largest stands of lettuce corals you'll ever see is in the middle of this pass. Anemones nestle inside and, at night, beautiful basket starfish come out and catch particles in the current from the edge of the coral lips.

Ngerumekaol averages about 50 to 60 feet but can get as deep as 80 in some spots. It is normally an ideal second dive and an exciting night dive as well.

Sea fans at Siaes Tunnel

Many divers prefer to drift out and go along the wall past the mouth.

23) Siaes Tunnel
Location: West of Ulong
Attractions: Huge, coral filled cavern
Depth Range: 80 to 130 feet

The Siaes Tunnel, located along Palau's outer barrier reef west of the Ulong Channel, is one of the most exciting dives these islands have to offer. It was found quite by accident by one of Francis Toribiong's guides a few years ago. A gaping cavern known for its sheer wall and active marine life, this mammoth underground cave is the home for a multitude of sea inhabitants from wispy black coral trees to sleeping sharks.

The tunnel entrance is not visible from the surface. Boats normally anchor in about 15 feet of water at the dropoff. The diver drifts down through the resident population of pyramid butterflyfish and begins descent along this active wall.

Siaes Dropoff is a fine experience in

itself. The gorgonian fans in the hues of electric crimson and sun gold quiver in the current that runs gently along the wall. Schools of weighty bumphead parrotfish course the area, moving vertically along the cliff face. At around 60 feet, the entrance to the tunnel becomes apparent.

A delta of sand comes clearly into view at this point. Unlike most of the wall, which drops off to awesome depths, the bottom here is visible. At about 90 feet the mouth of the chasm is clear and inviting.

Exploring this tunnel is not child's play by any manner. At depths averaging 100 to 130 feet, the cave provides an experience that borders on the edge of safe sport diving. It is not unusual to see a large ray rising from the sandy bottom of the entrance. Inside, reef and whitetip sharks use the cave for a resting place. They can be approached closely if care is taken not to breathe too heavily. A school of jacks is usually present and swoops in to satisfy its collective curiosity past the diver's probing light. A Jewfish-sized grouper has also been reported here. The roof of the cave is forested in black coral, while the floor is covered in gorgonians.

Sharks also like to sleep in a side opening of the tunnel. This room, found to the right while exiting, is at a more respectable 100 feet and also has a window exit to the sea. A diver can swim to it using natural light, but a dive light is helpful here as well. The dark reaches are home to a moray eel and usually a sleeping leopard nurse shark. They are sometimes joined by whitetips.

Non-stinging jellies

The exit is made through a litter of large sea fans growing from the roof and the sides of the window and ascending up the wall for a safety deco stop.

24) Jellyfish Lake
Location: Eil Malk Island
Attractions: Marine Lake, jellyfish
Depth Range: 1 to 30 feet
Access: Hike, local guide

Ever since the marine lakes of Palau appeared in National Geographic magazine, the Jellyfish Lake of the Rock Islands has been a popular destination for snorkelers. Located deep in the islands, boats motor around nearly exposed coral patches to a shaded jungle cove. The water here holds giant tridacna clams that can be seen easily by snorkeling. A razor coral named after photographer Douglas Faulkner is also abundant here.

Surrounded by jellies

The excursion through the sharp, rocky limestone forest begins at the end of the cove. This has been aided with the construction of a dock and a blazing of a better trail in recent years as this has become a top tourist attraction. There is now a charge to see the lake and it goes toward maintaining the trail.

The hike to the lake is up a steep hill to the top of a Rock Island, then down the ridges to the edge of a briny swamp. Below, decaying vegetation mixes with a maze of roots. Small fish, blackbelted cardinalfish, dart in and out. A closer look will also reveal some small, white anemones with flowing tentacles lining the roots. These are the only enemies the jellyfish have as they will eat juvenile jellyfish.

To find the jellyfish, head for the sun. There are two type found here, the most prominent being the mastigias species. The animals have developed a symbiotic relationship with an algae.

Basically, the plant gets its energy from the sun and the jellyfish from the algae. Thus, the jellyfish seeks the sunlight to keep the algae producing. The animals have no need to sting as they have no enemies in this environment and they feed themselves. Thus, they are safe to touch. However, if you are extremely allergic, you should not do this as there are still some stinging cells in the water.

Depending upon the time of day, the jellyfish will be found in direct sunlight. As the sun narrows across the lake in the afternoon, the jellyfish move closer together and the snorkeler can expect to be surrounded by hundreds of thousands of jellies at all depths. It is a surreal experience.

Saltwater crocodile

The SOUTH

Two dropoffs have attracted photographers from around the world. Both are in the Ngemelis islands called Blue Corner and Big Dropoff. The entire southern end of the archipelago is blessed with world class wall diving, including impressive, coral-rich dropoffs and coral gardens.

25) Shark City
Location: Southwestern Barrier Reef
Attractions: Shark and 'cuda action
Depth Range: 20 to 120 feet

This is one of the best big fish dives in Palau. Shark City is a wall dive and drift dive and the sea fans, soft corals and other marine growth here is quite good. There are some very large and colorful sea anemones along the wall and also on the upper reef.

This point actually has four fingers where lots of good sea life viewing can take place. Each finger features a variety of marine life and also harbors some specific fish. One has a resident school of barracuda. One has a school of jacks. One is good for grey reef sharks. And there are big sea turtles here as well.

This is also one of those places that the occasional hammerhead and sailfish or marlin will stray into, so keep an eye on the blue water. Again, like most hot spots in Palau, the most big critter action will take place when the tide is moving, so time your dive accordingly.

It was named Shark City by Skin Diver publisher Paul Tzimoulis many years ago prior to the discovery of Blue Corner. For a long time, it was Palau's premiere dive. Now, it is not visited very often, which is a shame.

26) Ngerchong
Location: Southeastern Rock Islands
Attractions: Incoming action
Depth Range: 20 to 130 feet

This dive is often saved by Palau dive operators for the times when windy or stormy weather comes in from the west and closes out the more popular dive sites at Ngemelis and Peleliu. But it is a very rich and rewarding dive locale and should be done at incoming tide change for maximum results.

The dive starts on a sloping reef and divers may have to swim with a little energy to get over the reef edge, but after that a nice drift dive will take divers along a sculpted slope. The hill is highlighted by table corals, some beautiful and large gorgonian sea fans and lots of crannies and crevices that are home to lobsters, eels and small invertebrates like nudibranchs.

The water column is rich with schooling fish and the sloping wall eventually wall eventually leads to Ngerchong Channel, where the fish life at the mouth increases dramatically. Drifting along the water column, expect to see mackerel, occasional dogtooth tuna and lots of grey reef sharks that will approach a diver quite closely. Manta rays have also been observed coasting along the deeper reaches feeding easily in the currents.

At the reef, look for juvenile grey reef shark schools. A variety of different groupers live in the cascading shelves. Pufferfish have been seen mating at Ngerchong. The drift into the channel takes the diver past schools of jacks, black snappers, longnose barracudas and opens up a shallow shelf that can rise to as shallow as 20 feet. It is topped with large coral head. Look for sea

Palau Marine Lake

Snapper feeding at German Channel

turtles and banded sea snakes among a myriad of other reef life here.

27) German Channel
Location: North of Ngemelis Wall
Attractions: Giant clams, corals, manta rays and more
Depth Range: 20 to 120 feet

Heading north from the Ngemelis Wall toward the Rock Islands, divers pass an area of broad sand flats covered in 10 to 40 feet of water. The reflection from the white sand turns the sea to a bright shade of turquoise. This inviting area has been called the German Channel named after the cut the Germans blasted through reef to ease boat passage during their occupation of Palau from 1899 to 1914.

This vast expanse has a number of buoys and is heavily dived. It is also an anchorage area for many of Palau's live aboards. It is also a main passageway for boats, so divers should use a safety sausage here at all times and not surface quickly. Tide changes in Palau can mean a difference of seven feet at times. The water funneling over these flats into the depths of the open sea

Manta feeding at German Channel

reaches a respectable but not treacherous speed and the diver merely has to drop over the edge of the boat and go with the flow. The bottom appears to have been landscaped. Gorgonian fans with scarlet skeletons and snowy, white polyps quiver as they extend in the current. Crinoids in many hues abound on top of coral heads. Forests of staghorn coral thickets provide refuge for clouds of damselfish.

An observant diver can usually spot a cuttlefish in these thickets as well. They are curious by nature and they study a diver and react by flashing various hues of electric color. Also, the odd juvenile baramundi cod hovers over the corals.

Large triggerfish travel these flats, turtles like to sleep under the platter corals and sharks pass by frequently in the distance. Many spots also have garden eels.

The big attraction is big mantas that are known to arrive near the mouth of the Channel in fighter-like formation at tide change, also feeding on the nutrients in the current. They can also be seen in deeper water where there is a cleaning station. In the open water above the cleaning station one can see grey reef sharks and other pelagics. Sailfish swim in the shallows here high above the dropoff. Near these deeper sites are where the buoys have been

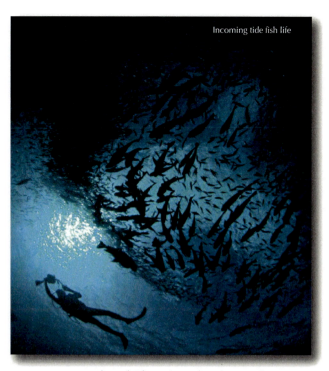

Incoming tide fish life

placed. There is a cleaning station near the dropoff and mantas will come to it if divers sit on the bottom and wait. They will also feed above this area, so look up into the shallow water as there may be action above your head.

28) Big Dropoff/Ngemelis Wall
Location: Ngemelis West Channel
Attractions: Sheer wall of life
Depth Range: 3 to 900 feet

One of the best known wall dives in sport diving lore is the Ngemelis Wall in southern Palau. Also called Big Dropoff, this sheer cut supports just about every form of marine life. Located just south of the historic German Channel, the dropoff starts in extremely shallow water (sometimes knee deep at low tide) and falls to depths greater than 900 feet. Just make a couple of kicks from the shallow reeftop over the inky abyss and free fall. Normally, a gentle current runs along the southeastern wall, which is the most frequented dive area. There is a large resident Napoleon wrasse here and a school of sergeant majors and yellowtails.

The wall has an abundance of sea fans at all depth levels. The deeper fans can reach nine feet across and come in hues of crimson and green. Crinoids sit on these fans to feed in the current and decorate them like holiday tinsel. It is also home to great barrel sponges and pretzel-like rope sponge formations. The fish population is also quite varied. Big schools of yellowtails course the wall vertically, seeming to spill into the water from above the reef. Look also for schools of parrotfish and a great abundance of pyramid butterflyfish. The crevices hold leaf fish and fire dartfish. This is also a great night dive with the tubastrea corals blossoming into fields of golden polyps.

The top of the wall is also rich in marine life with many sea anemones and clouds of chromis and small reef fish. Look for a red fluorescent sea anemone along the wall. Stunning.

29) Turtle Wall
Location: Ngemelis West Channel
Attractions: Sheer wall of life
Depth Range: 15 to 130 feet

This site located between the more famous dive of Big Dropoff and New Dropoff is known for its abundance of soft corals and gorgonian sea fans. As the name implies, it is a

Ngemelis Wall

popular gathering site for green and hawksbill sea turtles. As is the norm for this area, this is a drift dive that can run either east or west, depending on the currents. The wall is adorned with tubastrea and other smaller hard corals. More spectacular are the deeper sea fans and soft coral colonies. The crimson sea whips can also be seen.

For sea life, this place is quite good as it encompasses a corner of Ngemelis Island and the currents flowing from Big Dropoff carry lots of nutrients. Expect to see schools of rainbow runners, grey reef sharks, whitetip sharks, fusiliers and Napoleon wrasse.

There is a major plankton flow past this tip and some of the larger planktonic animals can be observed in the blue water. It is not unusual to see mantas feeding in the blue. This is also a good spot to see the occasional seasonal whale shark.

Entering at the Dropoff

30) New Dropoff
Location: West Ngemelis Wall
Attractions: Shark and 'cuda action
Depth Range: 20 to 120 feet

The name may not be the catchiest, but that doesn't detract from the excitement the marine life provides. For years, Palau's Blue Corner has been the premier attraction for dropoff divers, but this dive is also full of shark and barracuda action and features Napoleon wrasse, sea turtles and eagle rays as frequently seen critters. The site is located right around the corner from **Big Dropoff** and **Turtle Wall**, actually on the way to Blue Corner. The site is near the snorkeling area called **Fairyland** and another popular deep dive called **Virgin Blue Hole**. New Dropoff features starts in between 15 to 30 feet, depending where you jump in.

This area has a lot of currents, just like Blue Corner, and keeping oneself neutral can be a little unnerving when side currents, down currents and up currents are all bouncing you around. But once you get a handle on what is going on, you can stop and appreciate all sizes and kinds of fish. Use a reef hook to watch the action.

Schools of blue-stripe snappers and the larger grey snappers are common along the dropoff. Both sharpnose and blackbar barracuda are seen frequently. There are many cuts and corners where currents propel the diver. It is not unusual to go sweeping around a corner to within a few feet of silvery schooling 'cuda that are just hovering off the wall. A reef hook helps greatly if you want to stop and watch the fish action. This can be done in 45 to 60 feet of water, so the diver can stay here

Napoleon wrasse

quite a while.

Each diver usually reports seeing something special on this dive including patrolling grey reef sharks that approach quite closely, graceful hawksbill turtles and even a six-foot, leopard nurse shark swimming freely down the wall, out into open water, along the wall and back up again. Its swimming action is completely different from most sharks.

New Dropoff has its share of beautiful coral fans and soft corals as well. The wall is alive with small tropicals and sea anemones are found along the upper reaches of the drop. The dive ends at an area where much of the tidal flow exits the inner reef flats and can be a little murky. During normal conditions, visibility is about 80 feet along this wall.

New Drop is one of the bottomless dives that has made Palau famous, so it is wise to keep a good eye on your depth gauge and realize what you're doing. It is easy to get carried away swimming after a turtle or some other exotic marine animal here and find your dive profile completely botched.

31) Blue Corner
Location: SW Ngemelis Island
Attractions: Sensory Overload
Depth Range: 40 to 130 feet

Blue Corner off the Ngemelis islands is one of those dives that is consistently electric, providing fish action in every imaginable shape and size. Large sharks are common, as are small ones, sea turtles, groupers, schools of barracudas, snappers and small tropicals, Napoleon wrasse and bumphead parrotfish, and even an occasional moray eel or sea snake. Incredibly big stingrays have also been seen here. The site is world famous.

The amazing thing about Blue Corner is that about 90 percent of all of these animals are spotted on every dive. The Corner is an area of the reef flat that starts in about 45 feet of water and runs for a great distance, jutting out into the sea before dropping off abruptly to form a wall. Small hills, sand tunnels and gorges are cut into the upper side. A strong tidal current runs through, providing food for the bottom of the marine chain, which in turn attracts the middle and upper chain critters.

A typical dive starts by descending along the wall through schooling fish and at least a dozen reef sharks that are curious about the noise of the diver's bubbles. Prior to the tip is a cut in the wall that boasts immense and colorful gorgonian fans as well as feathery black coral trees. Look below for jacks.

Once up on the 50-foot level, the schools of fish that course the corner can be watched for hours. Using a reef hook is highly recommended here so the diver isn't grabbing coral and also it is much easier to watch the action.

Gray reef shark at Blue Corner

The Magic of Blue Corner

Barracuda school

Bigeye jacks at the Corner

Blue Corner was found by pioneer Francis Toribiong and his crew in the mid-1980s while venturing along the wall after a Blue Holes dives. Once explored and understood, it has become one of the most famous dive sites in the world. There are large bigeye jack, barracuda, snapper and shark schools roaming the area and moving with the changing currents. People can watch the ocean's opera perform in real time at a fairly shallow depth as an amazing amount of marine life lives off the southern Palau ocean point. Few places in the world provide consistent action and photo opportunities like Blue Corner.

Napoleon wrasse

Snapper school

Descending the Blue Holes

Gray reef shark

Bottom of Blue Holes

Some fish schools actually mix together, with as many as four different species swimming in one dense formation. Moving a little farther into an area of heavier coral growth, it is not unusual to see as many as a half-dozen hawksbill sea turtles grazing on hydroids.

Because it is so consistently active, Blue Corner has become a Mecca for world-class underwater photographers and should be considered a must for every serious diver. The currents here can be powerful and tricky at times. Be sure to watch for down and up currents that run along the walls that can bring a diver up or down faster than wanted and really mess with a dive profile. The sharks here are well-fed, but treat them with respect anyway, especially during mating season in May and June, when they can be more aggressive. It is during this time that schools of Moorish idols also swim along the wall and are actually herded to the surface by sharks and fed upon.

The deeper reaches of Blue Corner harbor a very large school of horse eye jacks. Bigger fish have also been reported in the blue water to include hammerhead and tiger sharks, marlin, sailfish and even schooling yellowfin tuna and leatherback sea turtles.

During high season, there can be many boats and divers here. The current almost always sweeps divers off the point upon ascent. For those major reasons, a dive should not be attempted here without a safety sausage.

32) The Blue Holes
Location: SW Ngemelis Island Reef
Attractions: Large, light-filled caverns
Depth Range: 10 to 130 feet

It is a popular practice to dive through Palau's Blue Holes and then make a drift dive to the Blue Corner, as they are very close to one another.
The Blue Holes are holes in the top of the reef flat that lead to four vertical shafts that open on the outer reef wall. The diver can descend here and then drift down the shafts, watching the sunlight play with the hues of blues as the refracted rays dance in the water.

The walls of the holes have tubastrea and wire corals. Black coral, or antipathes, grows sporadically, especially near the exit below. These corals don't especially like or need direct sunlight other corals require.

The dive is quite deep, with the first exit at about 85 feet. Down this deep, the water is a heavy blue that goes deeper and darker to the open sea. Incredibly large fish have been seen here, including some immense wahoo and tuna resembling silver Volkswagens.

The bottom is sandy. Spotted leopard nurse sharks have been known to rest here, allowing diver to approach very close before being coaxed from their resting spot. Whitetip sharks sleep here as well.

The diver can exit and when the current is right, drift all the way to Blue Corner, watching out for sharks and turtles on the way. Or it is easy to ascend and explore the outer wall, which has gorgonian sea fans and a rich violet soft coral. Macro life can be good with orangutan crabs in bubble corals. There is a cave at one end of the bottom of the holes called The Temple of Doom. This is for extremely experienced and cave-trained divers only and should not be entered without lights, guide, rope, back-up air, etc.

33) Barnum Wall
Location: Across from Big Dropoff
Attractions: Wall, resting turtles, fish
Depth Range: 10 to 130 feet

Turtle Cove

Palau's Ngemelis Wall, also known as Big Dropoff, is one of the most famed dives in the world. It is a sheer wall teeming with fish and covered with every coral imaginable.

Just a short ride across the Ngemelis Channel is one of the least known dives in the world, Barnum Wall, near Ngercheu Island. The wall here is not as extreme as Ngemelis and the diver can go down along a sloping decline. This slope features some relief areas full of corals. Big cracks and crevices provide a home for a number of marine critters and there are large platter corals that sometimes become resting places for a

Turtle Cove snapper school

lot of turtles.

The wall has sea fans, though not the immense size of that at Ngemelis, and large stands of leather corals with their soft, swaying tentacles that resemble anemones. Like many of Palau's spectacular reefs, Barnum starts in about three feet of water. Near the reeftop are crinoids in proliferation. They come in many hues, with some being brilliant combinations of evergreen, gold and black.

The many cracks and crevices attract large groupers and a number of sweetlips. Smaller reef fish like pyramid butterflies and schools of fusiliers are common.

When the seas are calm in southern Palau, it makes for a fine second dive and may provide some surprises.

34) Turtle Cove
Location: North of Peleliu
Attractions: Wall, blue hole
Depth Range: 5 to 130 feet

Across the Ngemelis Channel is an area fondly known as Turtle Cove. This is a popular rest stop. There is a shaded beach and good snorkeling at the cove and after the proper surface interval a blue hole/wall dive is very handy. There are two buoys here. One is near the Turtle Cove blue hole and the other, farther east, usually has an immense school of striped yellow snapper and goatfish swirling in a bright yellow ball near its anchor point. This school is great for snorkeling and also good for photographers to take nice, colorful fish pictures.

Blacktip reef sharks

The hole sits atop the shallow reef flat. At low tide, it is possible to stand at the edge of the hole with part of your body still out of the water. The next step is the fun part. Drifting through this hole, one sees red and yellow soft coral trees in about 30 feet of water, although they used to be more abundant. Divers carelessly falling and kicking their fins have destroyed many of the delicate soft corals. The marine environment is fragile. Treat it with care.

The inside of the hole is honeycombed with exits at various depths. One small passage is the home for a family of large lionfish. They have lived in this little cave for years and are occasionally joined by a grouper. Drifting farther down, a large window opens to the outer wall at only 70 feet. All along this area are elegant, golden sea fans and wispy black coral trees. A leopard nurse shark sometimes sleeps on the bottom.

This bottom then slopes down to about 90 feet and falls off to more than 200. But the outer wall rises to near the surface on both sides and a swim along it will bring good wall activity. There are fans of burgundy and cream adorned with flowing crinoids. Fluted oysters also display their kaleidoscopic mantles until scared shut by a burst of bubbles.

Schools of fusiliers and tiger-striped sweet-lips add to the fish action. The wall ends at a point and grey reef sharks and fish schools can be found here at incoming tide. Also, keep a lookout for Titan triggerfish nests.

35) Matthew's Place
Ngercheu Garden
Location: South of Turtle Cove
Attractions: Hard Corals and unusual fish, good night dive
Depth Range: 20 to 90 feet

This wonderful protected cove is great for a casual dive and for poking around looking for the odd and unusual, especially at night. This is an area of heavy hard coral cover with castle corals, acropora and table corals all sharing space on a healthy reef.

Peleliu WWII memorial

Named for former guide Matthew Elebelau, it was his favorite spot to find resting turtles and colorful tropical fish.

At night, this area is generally free of currents and slopes so dives at depths of anywhere from 20 to 80 feet can be made. Some amazing night sites have been seen here including a slumbering giant bumphead parrotfish with a cadre of cleaner shrimps scouring its face and the elusive and comical firefish. The firefish is a member of the lionfish family but actually kind of scurries across the reef floor. Also, look here for shells, shrimps and sleeping parrotfish.

36) Peleliu Wall and Tip
Location: Southern Peleliu Island
Attractions: High voltage drift diving
Depth Range: 20 to 130 feet

The southern tip of the island of Peleliu in the Palau archipelago provides a dive that is a true example of sensory overload. It is wild, open ocean where current from both sides of this huge archipelago converge. The richness of Palau's waters is truly evident from the first drop in the water.

The terrain around this end of Peleliu plunges abruptly to at least 900 feet. There is a shallow shelf that extends from the shore covered by 10 to 15 feet of water, but it ends at an abrupt drop in the form of a coral covered wall that is alive with marine life. Normally, sharks are a fact of life along this wall. There are also turtles, sea snakes, large groupers and schools of mastiff bumphead parrotfish.

In the area, huge gorgonians of all colors grow in as little as 25 feet of water and extend to the depths, seeming to grow in size as they descend. Feathery black coral trees with thick bases appear occasionally and soft corals, with electric royal purple polyps, adorn the outcrops.

Brown barrel sponges are home to white sea cucumbers that like to hide in the sponge's folds. Many kinds of porifera live on the wall. There are also cuts and crevices to explore that are painted with encrusting sponges and tunicate colonies. This entire wall is best enjoyed by dropping far back and doing a drift to the Peleliu Tip. The current will normally increase as one approaches the tip.

The tip area sits in 30 to 50 feet of water and a reef hook is advised here. It is possible to finish the dive here and watch all of the pelagic action that often includes marlin and occasional tiger sharks.

One note of caution, the up current as one approaches the tip can shoot a diver upwards 40 feet in a matter of seconds and take a diver down just as quickly. This is a place to be vigilant or time and depth. The current is also swift at the surface at times. Make sure your boat driver knows you are up. Always carry a safety sausage so you don't wind up floating to the Philippines. Listen to your guide's briefing very carefully here and do what he or she recommends to ensure the boat gets you in a timely manner and in safe waters.

If you do venture past the tip, the reef gets deeper quickly and coral cover disappears as this is the other side of the finger and there isn't so much to see.

These few concerns aside, which are just common sense when diving where two ocean currents meet, enjoy the exciting dive. Peleliu Wall has to rank as one of the world's finest sport dives.

37) Yellow Wall
Location: SE end of Peleliu Island
Attractions: Wall & Reef Dive
Depth Range: 40 to 130 feet

Aptly named for the thousands of tube coral polyps that blossom in the flowing current and make this outer reef wall glow in a golden yellow hue, Yellow Wall is a great variety dive. It

Film maker Al Giddings in WWII Peleliu cave

can be done in many ways. Starting near Honeymoon beach, the wall drops off steeply and the current normally carries toward the southern tip. The wall here has a number of pock marks and cuts, arches and overhangs that are all adorned in sea life. One arch in particular is covered in the Yellow Wall polyps and makes a great backdrop for a model to swim into.

There are also a lot of hydroids growing here that sea turtles enjoy feeding on so keep an eye out for these undersea reptiles. The current will increase as one approaches the end of the island. To avoid getting swept away, swim up top to observe life in the coral gardens. Here schools of sweetlips, snappers and emperors can be found. Look for eels in the coral heads and large groupers under the table corals.

38) Pelelliu Express
Location: SE Peleliu Island
Attractions: High voltage drift diving
Depth Range: 60 to 130 feet

Some people swear by this dive and others swear at it. That is because it is a major drift dive, rather deep and out into oblivion. Why do it? The chance of seeing Mr. Big is the enticement. The southern end of Peleliu has a finger that juts out into the sea and it swept by currents. Large pelagic fish including ocean-going whitetip sharks, grey reefs, bronze whalers, sailfish, marlin and other rarely seen fish show up here.

This dive is sometimes combined with a Yellow Wall dive as the two run into one another. There are places to hook on to the reef along the expressway

Santa Maria Point

Santa Maria Point soft corals

and watch for fish action. Normally, grey reef sharks are constant companions. Dogtooth tuna, sometimes in schools, Spanish mackerel and albacore tuna are also seen.

As this ride is current-swept, the reef does not have a lot of growth. Sea whips bend in the current and the tougher hard corals pop up from the reef base. This is another of those dives where a safety sausage and good surface conditions are a must before attempting this wild ride in the sea. Decompression is done floating in open ocean. This can be a dangerous dive so only go when seas are calm.

39) Angaur/Santa Maria Point
Location: Southern archipelago
Attractions: Pelagics, schooling fish
Depth Range: 20 to 100 feet

Angaur is not dived much by sport divers because the open ocean crossing between Peleliu and Angaur must be attempted only when weather is very calm. The channel between the two islands can be very rough and the wave action on the western shores can be notable as well.

One place people dive is at the Santa Maria Point along the northeast shore. Actually, there is a Catholic shrine to the Blessed Virgin, a Buddhist monument and a Shinto Shrine, so this is also a popular corner for religions, including SCUBA worshippers.

This site slopes quickly to 90 feet and offers some extremely clear water. Angaur is the top of a submerged mountain, so it rises from the sea with little in the way of protective fringing reef. The wave action here is intense. Thus, the coral heads are small at reeftop. Down deeper, expect to see sea fans and lots of fish. The schools can be quite large at times with a mixture of pelagic fish including whale sharks and even oceanic whitetips and tiger sharks. Also off Angaur, for tek wreckies, the quite deep **USS Perry** shipwreck is ready for TriMix divers.

Bull sharks come to predate on the spawning red snappers.

Full Moon Fever

The more people dive around Palau the more they find out about the ways of Nature and Mother Ocean. Local sea knowledge has grown over the years, the rich traditional fishing community knows much about the spawning cycles of many of the food fish and scientists are more prevalent in Palau and learning more and more about cyclical events. And, to the benefit of divers, these events can now be experienced through some of the local dive shops that focus on the natural occurrences.

For instance, at Sam's Tours trips to these events are now organized on a regular basis. They aren't always as convenient as a leisurely 9 a.m. to 4 p.m. dive day trip. Sometimes it means getting up well before dawn to travel to the sites that feature spawning aggregations. Currents can be fierce due to the moon phase and there's no guarantee the weather will be sunny and the seas flat. However, rewards can be high.

For several days leading up to and around the full moon, two huge known aggregations of red snappers (Lutjanus bohar) aggregate, ready to spawn in two different locations. One is off the historical island of Peleliu and the other to somewhat remote dive sites east of Koror. Usually divers' preferences and weather condition determine which site will be visited.

As the sun rises, divers begin the dive to watch the spectacle that is about to unfold. A huge aggregation of snapper rises from the deep in a spawning mass to ensure the continuation of their species. Witnessing this natural behavior, which has been described as an underwater fireworks display of energy and excitement, has an added bonus. This amazing action brings in the biggest predators in Palau like massive bull sharks and hammerheads. It is a special time in the sea.

Snapper aren't the only mating fish at center stage. Bumphead parrotfish (Bolbometopon muricatum), the big coral-crunching parrots that roam the reef in small schools and sometimes individually, also have a mating activity in Palau that is massive in size and is rarely seen anywhere else.

Bumpheads are often seen patrolling the reefs in schools of up to 20 or more but when the mating starts in Palau the aggregation can mean nearly a thousand individuals!

The New Moon Expedition goes to a remote dive site where aggregations begin forming early in the morning. Awaiting the exact time for spawning, hundreds of bumpheads from all around the area join one another. Building up to this spectacular showdown, males begin their display of dominance, attempting to attract as many mating partners as possible. As females continue to gather, the school spills out into the blue where the tension erupts into a climatic mating dance. The huge parrotfish fly through the blue with great speed.

The trips are led by Paul Collins, an active marine researcher in Palau with a master's degree in Marine Science, Paul has worked in and around the dive industry in Palau for years. He has been able to build a picture of these locations that he hopes will help him understand why these spectacular events happen at these special locations. His partner is Richard Barnden, a gifted photographer who also has an addiction in animal behavior and spawning aggregations. To join them contact Unique Dive Expeditions' Reservations Desk at **uniquediving@samstours.com.** There are also manta feeding occurrences, Moorish idol mating, grouper spawning and shark mating events.

The huge congregation of bumphead parrotfish mating is a Palau special event.

Kaday Village greeting

Anthias & anemone at Yap Caverns

Yap, Micronesia

Yap is the traditional Micronesian island that is just a little over an hour away from Guam but worlds away in terms of culture. In the last couple of years, Yap has made cautious but progressive steps to cash in on Micronesia's growing popularity as a holiday destination. The result is a convenient adventure' of sorts. Just a little over an hour from bustling Guam, the jet lands and you're in a very special islandy place.

Tradition plays an important role in life on the islands of Yap. The people here are very proud of their unique culture and have resisted major changes and modernization. The pavement ends as one leaves the town and heads to the villages. Here life continues much as it has for hundreds of years.

Yap's history dates back to about 200 AD but may go farther as there have not been that many archaeological studies about these unique island people. Evidence on Map island shows the 200 AD date.

They have been known well as great ocean navigators. Those residents of the outer atolls still sail vast distances in open canoes hewn from the immense trunks of breadfruit trees. Each ocean-going canoe is built by hand using adzes and other manual carving tools. Outboards have taken the place of these great canoes on some islands, but outer islanders in this atoll state still keep the tradition going strong.

Sunrise in Yap

East coast meeting house

Today, Yap state consists of the main high islands of Yap proper (Wa'ab) and the outer islands (Remetau). A strong caste system was once in effect, with the higher castes living in the villages of the high islands. These castes are still followed loosely today, but have broken down over the years and the chiefs do not posses absolute power as they once did.

Yapese dress is still traditional, not so much in town but in the small villages. Men still wear loincloths and women wear grass skirts or lava-lavas. If you are visiting, women should wear clothing that covers the thigh. Toplessness is not considered offensive on Yap, but a woman in a miniskirt is shocking. Things are a little more lax in the main town in Colonia and on boats.

Village stone path

Village pool game

A guide s handy but not mandatory. Permission must be asked of each village chief before entering the area and a local guide can smooth things over considerably. Yapese, some Japanese and English are spoken but Yapese is the main language of the people.

If there is a celebration scheduled, it is worth watching. History, legends and stories are passed down by word of mouth and through song. Old and new songs and dances are performed at celebrations and are quite colorful and melodic. Yap Day, which is actually a three-day celebration of dances and other traditions, is always March 1.

Geography

Yap is part of the Federated States of Micronesia. The entire state consists of scattered atolls. The capital island, called Yap Proper, is actually five islands of old volcanic origin surrounded by a huge barrier reef and connected by mangrove-lined waterways and manmade bridges. As the outer islands are minimally developed and hard to reach, most diving is done in Yap Proper.

Yap's southern tip features steep ocean walls and deep reef canyons. The north has broad and sloping coral reef flats that fall gradually into the sea. Yap has many deep channels that provide unique diving experiences. It is in these channels that manta rays are frequently observed.

Climate

Yap's climate, like most of Micronesia, is also uniformly warm and humid. The

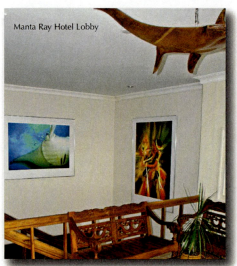
Manta Ray Hotel Lobby

evening temps average 72F (22C) in the evenings and 86F (31C) during the day. Dry season and trade wind season runs from late December to May. Rainfall averages 120 inches a year, but is seasonal. The heaviest rains tend to occur in the summer months while the winter and spring trade wind season (marked by strong east to northeast winds) is relatively dry

Getting There

Currently, travellers must then connect to Yap via Guam or Manila through United Airlines, which has only a few flights weekly to Yap.

Getting Around

Taxis are cheap and plentiful for getting around town. Colonia is small, so walking is also advisable and pleasant. To travel to the outer villages, it is best to rent a car while visiting. There are locally-owned rental agencies. It is best to reserve a car through your hotel before you arrive to ensure you will get one.

Language

There are four indigenous languages in Yap: Yapese, Ulithian, Woleian and Satawalese. English is the official language of the FSM and is commonly spoken and understood. Many elderly Yapese are fluent in Japanese.

Entry

A valid passport and ongoing airline ticket are necessary for entry to Yap. Visas are not required for tourists for visits of up to 30 days. EAll visitors must have an onward or return ticket. 96941.

Health Care

Yap State Government operates a 150 bed hospital that is well stocked and professionally staffed. Intensive care and treatment serious injuries must be conducted off island. There is a small, one-person diving chamber. Dengue fever has been a problem and visitors should use mosquito repellent in the evenings.

Time

Yap is located on the western side of the international dateline. Coming from points east you lose a day when crossing the international dateline. Yap is 10 hours ahead of GMT/UTC. When its noon on Yap and Rota it is 6 pm the day before in San Francisco.

Electricity

Electricity is 110/120 volts, 60 cycle and the flat, two-pronged plug is used, same as in the USA.

Weights & Measures

The imperial system of measurement is used. Distances: inches, feet, yards, miles. Weights: ounces, pounds, tons. Air on scuba gauges is read in pounds and underwater depth is read in feet. See the conversion table in the back of the book.

What to Bring

It never gets cold in Yap, so only lightweight clothing should be brought. Attire is very casual and formal wear is considered unnecessary and impractical. (A former Governor once proposed establishing a low forbidding the wearing of ties in Yap!)

For Men will find slacks and a Hawaiian style shirt appropriate for even the most formal occasion in Yap. For women, lightweight cotton dresses blouses and skirts make the best island wear. Longer shorts, lavalavas and slacks are also acceptable attire.

Dive Related Equipment

Yap has a good basic assortment of equipment. If a personal piece of dive gear should fail, it is possible to replace it through rental or purchase. Repairs and parts are limited. Yap Divers has a facility called Manta Visions that has camera rental and instruction.

Money and Credit Cards

Credit Cards are taken at most hotels and a very limited number of stores and restaurants. Have some US currency on hand for purchases. There is an ATM in town. The official currency in Yap is the US Dollar. Yap is famous for its Stone Money which is still in use for traditional exchanges such as the purchase of traditional land.

Yap Visitor's Bureau

www.visityap.com
Tel: (691)350-2298
yvb@mail.fm

Yap Sunset

Yap Dive Sites

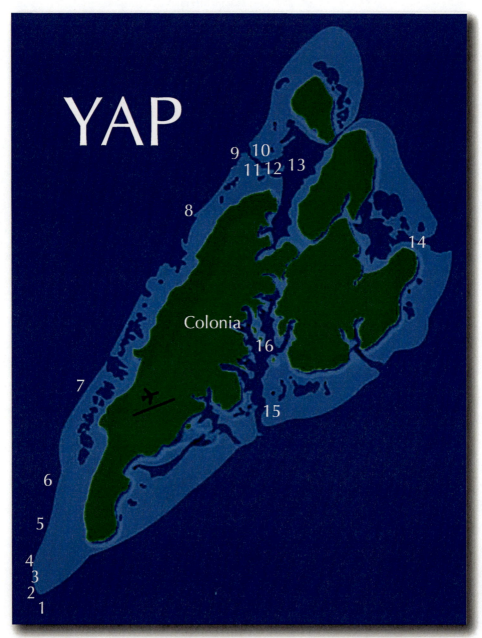

Yap Dive Sites

1) Gilman Tip
2) Lionfish Wall
3) Yap Caverns
4) Gilman Wall
5) Magic Kingdom
6) Spanish Walls
7) Cherry Blossom Wall
8) Vertigo
9) Yap Corner
10) Spaghetti Factory
11) Manta Ridge
12) Deep Cleaning Station
13) Stammitsch
14) Gofnuw
15) Slow & Easy
16) Rainbow Reef

Diving in Yap

Yap has two types of diving. The outer reefs feature some of the healthiest and most diverse hard corals of anywhere in the Pacific. The eastern shore has large coral gardens with big coral formations and interesting small invertebrate marine life. The western side of the island features sheer dropoffs, a cavern system and big pelagic life, like schools of barracuda, bumphead parrotfish and reef sharks.

The second is the channel diving. The inner channels of Yap are famous as a home for a resident school of manta rays. For best visibility, dive with the high, incoming tide. At low tide, visibility can decrease as nutrients wash into the channels from the nearby mangroves, but the mantas still can be seen most of the time at cleaning stations. But it is most dramatic to see them come in from the clear blue and approach ever so close.

The Walls and Reefs

1) Gilman Tip
Location: Gilman Tip
Attractions: Pelagics, fish schools, coral
Depth: 20 to 130 feet

Yap offers some nearly virgin dive opportunities on reefs as well as walls. The Gilman Tip is one such spot. Located at the southern end of Yap's barrier reef, the Gilman area shows little sign of being affected by man. This is seen in the intense and undamaged coral growth and the large numbers of fish that display an innocent curiosity when divers approach. This tip juts out more than two miles from the Yap mainland, representing the southernmost point on the barrier reef.

This site has always been popular with fishermen and divers alike. It is a dropoff area located and the southern tip of the Yap barrier reef where two currents converge and flow out to open

Gilman Reeftop

ocean. The fish and pelagic action here is usually quite good to spectacular. Molamolas (ocean sunfish), orcas, dolphin schools and whales sharks have all been seen trying to dine on the fish frappe that convenes when the currents are running off this point.

More often than not, the dives are drift dives. Look for schools of huge bumphead parrotfish, sleeping whitetip sharks, reef gray sharks, moray eels, rotund groupers, a school of copper sweepers, large triggerfish along the upper reef and a kaleidoscope of tropical fish in an incredible variety of hues and colors.

Gilman Tip offers a breathtaking sheer vertical face covered with a rich array of hard and soft coral and gorgonian corals. This is a place to see golden and multicolored crinoids on top of sea fans and on top of coral heads. At times, pilot whales have also been spotted here. For pristine coral and good fish watching, the Gilman Tip has a lot to offer. But the currents can be fierce. Make sure you have a safety sausage and go only when the guides deem in sane and worthy.

2) Lionfish Wall
Location: Gilman Tip
Attractions: Crannies and crevices with lionfish, fish schools
Depth: 20 to 130 feet

This dive can be done anywhere from 20 to 130 feet with bottom coming up at around 120 in some places. The best bet is around the 50 foot level,

Leaf fish at Lionfish Wall

Anemonefish & soft corals

however. Sleeping sharks seen frequently along the bottom. Big groupers can be spotted along with snappers, and lots and lots of bigeyes and soldierfish in the crevices.

Lionfish, especially the incredibly beautiful Pterois volitans with its white, flowing appendages, hide in the holes and under the ledges of the wall. They feed on small crabs and shrimps and they can inflict a painful sting.

Remember, they will stand their ground, so don't harass them. Another member of the scorpionfish family, the leaf fish, is found at about 20 feet near the top of Lionfish Wall where the Yap Caverns begin. There are usually others off the Caverns near the wall next to the anemones at 60 feet. This little fish looks like a leaf blowing in the current, except that it doesn't float away. It may also be colored red, black or a silvery white. Look for juveniles in the holes near the adults.

Large anemones, including a big cluster of bulb anemones, cling to the wall's sides. The reeftop is good for decompressing. Look for the big boxfish that sometimes swim in groups of three or more. The current can quickly change here, making it necessary to reverse directions but it is normally an easy drift.

3) Yap Caverns
Location: Near Gilman Tip
Attractions: White, sandy bottom
Depth: 20 to 70 feet

The most scenic area of this tip, a place called Yap Caverns, is where the whitetips snooze. The Lionfish Wall gives way to an undersea valley punctuated by

Yap Caverns

imposing, Medusalike coral heads. The floor of this site is in about 65 feet of water sloping upward to about 20 feet. The floor of the area is covered in snowy white sand. A quiet and slow approach will allow divers to sometimes observe whitetip sharks lazing about near overhangs and along the sandy slopes.

There are cleaning stations at some spots in this sandy maze atop the many coral heads. Deeper off the caverns is also some worthy diving. Sea anemones with purple tips at 80 feet with commensal shrimp and one-stripe clownfish can be found.

There are as many as 20 gray reef sharks at 90 feet near northwest side of the caverns. They mate and gestate in May and June and the males can be extremely aggressive and put on quite a display when the females are around, giving divers an action-packed and little bit scary show. There is also a shark cleaning station out there.

At times, there are baby sharks swimming within the protection of the larger sharks, similar to the way a pod of dolphins protects its young. To be able to see this kind of behavior of marine animals in the wild is one of the truly unique things Yap has to offer.

Along the wall are also some soft, branching corals. Look for ornate ghost

Dolphins off Gilman Wall

pipefish in May through July. The like to hide in the branches of the corals and also gain camouflage with the crinoids that are attached to the soft corals.

Cabbage Corals

The caverns themselves are also home to a huge "herd" of bumphead parrotfish. If you're the first divers there in the morning you may see them as they sleep in the protection of the cracks and crevices of the canyons.

The various caves and tunnels are great fun to swim through as most are well-lit tunnels that are easy to pass through. Starfish and copper sweepers hide inside the holes.

This is also a very good place to do photography, with rays of sun peeking through the canyons and cracks in the back of the cavern near the reef.

4) Gilman Wall
Location: North of Yap Caverns
Attractions: Big Crevices, coral formations
Depth: 20 to 100 feet

This dive is found at the north end of the Yap Caverns and features lots of big crevices. Turtles are often found swimming or resting here. On one encounter, I was swimming up a broad, wide crevice looking for invertebrates to practice some macrophotography with when a 7-foot moray eel came right out of its hole and was free swimming right at me. It was a little unnerving until it made an abrupt turn and disappeared into a hole in front of me.

The beautiful clown triggerfish is found here as the wall becomes more sloped. This also is a good spot for sea anemones Look for yellow tubastrea corals and small yellow encrusting sponges. This is a lively place with lots of fish when the tide is strong.

Mating nudibranchs

Anemonefish

a shelf at about 50 feet and then sloping again to about 110 feet. Then, the coral becomes sparse at about 120 feet and is so beautiful that diving in the 30 to 60 foot range should be the norm.

On the upper reaches of the tip, branching corals are abundant. Pyramid butterflyfish frequent these patches and light up the reef as their white and gold colors flicker to and fro in the gentle surge. Hovering above, close to the surface, are thick schools of sharpnose barracuda. Schools of the larger, black striped great barracuda also come in to peer at divers before returning to the blue water.

Some Medusalike coral heads, covered with bright encrusting sponges and plating corals, dot the reef landscape. Flowing formations of lettuce corals house blue damsels. Brain and other acropora grow into and over one another in competition for prime feeding space.

An occasional whitetip shark will coast by or can be seen resting on a coral ledge. Looking at the coral heads, one can see plenty of macro subjects for photography including shrimp at a cleaning station, tunicate colonies and yellow and black crinoids with their squat lobsters for macro buffs are propped on top of the lettuce corals.

5) The Magic Kingdom
Location: Southern Coastline
Attractions: Intense coral, fish schools
Depth: 20 to 90 feet

Fish and coral life here is healthy and active. Expect to see fish and reptiles like barracuda or batfish schools, sea turtles, whitetip and blacktip sharks and fusiliers in big numbers. The corals here are hard corals for the most part and very interesting, with many formations and mini-castles.

The reef slopes gently, planing off with

Purple anemone

6) Spanish Walls
Location: SW-central west coast
Attractions: Lace corals, overhangs, and fish schools
Depth: 20 to 100 feet

This site starts with divers descending on acres and acres of staghorn coral starting in about 25 feet of water and sloping down past 80 feet. In the branches of the coral are carpets of silver chromis that hover above catching food in the current. Many different sea anemones are also nestled in with a variety of clownfish darting in and out of the maze.

The geography then turns to masses of plate corals cascading down and punctuated by huge overhangs. Under these ledges lie groupers, bigeyes and squirrelfish. There are gorgonian fans growing in the cratered holes and

Spotted goby

tunnels of the formations and delicate lace corals also accent the sponge-encrusted site.

The diver will be impressed by the schools of fusiliers that seem to course by one after another at the start of this dive. The diver actually swims along a slope rich in coral growth before getting to the Spanish Walls, named so for their many lace corals resembling Spanish lace. Flashy blue fusiliers and the brilliant yellowtail fusiliers run up and down the reef, making for great photo opportunities.

It is not unusual for school of barracuda to come in for a look when divers start the dive. Be alert, or they may come and go without you knowing it. Glance occasionally into the blue beside you as well as looking ahead.. Reef whitetip sharks sleep on the hard corals here as well and at the wall will swim 20 or 30 feet under the diver. There are large cascading falls of plate corals at 70 feet at the walls. Soft corals and lace corals grow in the pocked overhangs following the dive along the rich slope. The corals are pastel colors and can be seen by swimming up inside the wall. Watch your bubbles, however, as they can be abrasive to the soft coral. It is impressive after leaving the Spanish Walls. There is lots of fish life shallow so safety decompression is entertaining. A lot of images can be shot here on the fish life.

7) Cherry Blossom Wall
Location: South central Yap
Attractions: Fusiliers, lace corals, and crevices
Depth: 30 to 110 feet

This place was named for the many flower coral colonies on fairly sheer wall, which gives it the look of blossoming. Each crook and crevice holds surprises. There are Christmas tree

Gray reef school

Diver & gray reefs

worms of various sizes and shapes littered all over some coral heads. The tiny invertebrates come in colors of shocking blue and outrageous yellow and multi-colors like a Baskin-Robbins swirl. There are some nice, violet lace corals hiding in some of the holes in the wall, making them a little tough to photograph, but not hard to observe and appreciate.

As a matter of fact, this is a good macrophotography spot. The top of the wall is nice for fish watching and there are some large anemones here. In the distance, the buffalo of the reef, or bumphead parrotfish, frolic in the upper reaches, munching coral and spewing sand.

8) Vertigo
Location: North east Yap
Attractions: Gray Reef Sharks
Depth: 20 to 130 feet

Yap is a great place to watch the higher end of the food chain. The waters and reef areas hold gray reef sharks, silky sharks, silvertips, whitetips, leopard sharks and blacktips. One rare occasions even whale sharks, oceanic whitetips and tiger sharks are seen in these waters.

Vertigo Reef is becoming Micronesia's premiere place to observe gray reef sharks coursing the blue and up close and personal. This is a reef where an occasional shark feed takes place. So the sharks show up for the heck of it when they hear a dive boat approach the reef. Large grays and the occasional blacktip move eerily in the water column. As many as a dozen sharks can be seen appearing in the blue out of nowhere. They may stay with divers for part or the entire dive along this sheer wall.

If there is a shark feed taking place,

Vertigo shark pack

Manta and Diver in Miil Channel

Manta getting cleaned

The Mantas and Miil Channel

Yap's big boast to the diving world is its regular manta sightings. For many years, Yap's fishermen hunting for a fish dinner near the Miil Channel, reported frequent sightings of manta rays swimming by their boats. Fortunately, mantas are not considered a delicacy in Yap, so they were not hunted.

When diving opened up through Yap Divers in 1987, Bill Acker and his crew went to explore this talk and sure enough, there were times when there were truly manta rays everywhere. It has taken years of observation to figure out the mantas' habits and produce methods that allow the average sport diver to observe them without disturbing the animal's natural routine. But this has become a reality and Yap proudly offers the diver regular sightings of these wonderful creatures that can rarely be seen elsewhere.

Gray reef shark at Yap Corner

Remember, don't chase the sharks or they will retreat out into the open water. Just find a good spot anda shark or many sharks will come by very close in camera range for some good shark shots.

If you are not doing a feed, that sharks will leave after maybe 20 to 30 minutes and you can dive the hard corals along the wall and slopes leading away from the Vertigo dropoff.

Bumphead parrotfish like the hard corals of the upper reef in the 30 to 600 foot range. Big puffers come in here as well. Also schools of tangs maraud along the reef finding algae patches to attack. The same with large groups of parrotfish. There's a lot to do and see at Vertigo.

those numbers very quickly quadruple. Sharks will be wary at first, but if challenged by hungry snappers, big morays and pack of sargeant majors, the sharks will start coming in to get bites of bait, which is usually tuna heads and parts left over from sashimi at one of the island's hotels.

This kind of reef excitement starts to get the attention of other big predators. Giant groupers have come up from the depths and schools of large rainbow runners swim by to see what is happening during the shark feed. This is one of the best places in the world to get great gray reef shark photos as the water on the deep outer wall is normally clear and blue.

The CHANNELS

Yap's outer reefs have numerous dive sites, but a lot of diving in Yap is done in deep, inner reef channels that are found on both the east and west coasts of the island. It is here a lot of water and nutrients move from the mangrove-lined lagoons to the open sea. This attracts Yap's most famous residents, the mantas. But these protected inner reef areas also are home to eagle rays, sharks, fish schools and lots of amazing macro life. Visibility is normally tide and surf driven. And the great variety of fish show up with the tide changes.

At Right: Miil Channel with Yap Corner

9) Yap Corner
Location: Mill Channel Mouth
Attractions: Sleeping sharks, fish schools, manta rays
Depth: 30 to 130 feet

This dive is best done on a morning incoming tide and usually offers plenty of pelagic and schooling action. Divers usually drop in at a point outside the Miil Channel mouth on the north side. There is a point here covered in coral and when the incoming tide sweeps in and over the reef, the current beckons lot of fish.

This point has variety of corals on the top reef, as well as a large number of anemones in deeper water. There are also many crinoids in many colors hanging on to the hard corals. The point cascades down into deep water in a series of steps. At about 110 feet, there is an undercuts with beautiful crimson sea whips inside. Look here also for a school of bigeye jacks that

Barracuda at Yap Corner

like to use this small cavern as refuge.

When the clear water of the open sea is coming in, visibility can reach well ver 100 feet and the huge expanse of this massive channel mouth is very impressive. Out in the blue divers will see gray reef sharks, including juveniles closer to the reef, snapper schools, eagle rays in schools or individually, rainbow runners, bigeye jacks, longnose and chevron barracuda and plenty more.

The channel floor usually has a very large school of the longnose barracuda. This is deep and can be deceptive so watch your time and depth and air if you head down to chase them for a photo.

Manta rays coming in to Miil Channel to be cleaned or to feed swoop in from the blue and gracefully swim into the channel here as well.

Rainbow runners at Yap Corner

Hawksbill

Mantas glide slowly overhead

Photographing Mantas

The mantas reside in these channels because the waters are rich in nutrients... which is great for mantas but not so swell for photographers. Just as silt causes backscatter problems on shipwrecks, the planktonic matter in the channels is also highly reflective.

The second problem is the animals themselves. Their backs are normally dark gray to black, while their undersides are snow white. To bring out their natural colors without making their bellies shine like the moon and their surroundings appear to be stars in the sky, I suggest you power down.

Expose for the ambient light and use the strobes as fill for color. Shooting with the strobe at one-half power or even one-quarter power is quite helpful in that it reduces the scatter problem, fills in the white of the belly to give a nice, natural appearance in the photos. It also doesn't take as long to recycle, which is important as the mantas do come close, but they don't always stay for a long time, so shoot fast and a lot.

Also, stay low and stay put and breath easy. The mantas will simply disappear if chased or touched. You can virtually kiss your manta shooting good-bye if you start swimming after them. They are curious and will come your way sooner or later. Also, a slow, controlled bubble exhalation will help keep them around.

If you want to see fish schools, I suggest a somewhat different dive plan. Just swim off the reef and up into the blue water directly over the floor of the channel. Hanging in the blue void you will see schools of barracuda, schools of large and long rainbow runners and lots of other open ocean fish like Spanish mackerel or even a wahoo. Many times people get impatient and start swimming into the channel with the tide, which is fine. But an entire dive can be done by just hanging out at various depths around the corner itself.

The upper reef follows a slope with huge star and brain coral heads. Here there is always a resident school of black snappers. Look also for feeding bumphead parrotfish and a couple of beautiful aqua Napoleon wrasses. Small critters also like the corals and cracks. There are more crinoids with the commensal like-colored squat lobsters and clingfish.

10) Miil Channel Spaghetti Factory
Location: Miil Channel
Attractions: Sea fans, sea whips, shark cleaning station and wall cuts
Depth: 20 to 130 feet

If you want to take a drift in through the Grand Canyon of the Pacific, you can start at the Spaghetti Factory and explore some fascinating channel, reef and canyon wall life assisted by the gentle ride of an incoming tide.

100-foot walls loom on both sides, but keeping the reef on the left seems to have the most life. This is a good place to come set up for macro photography, although there is plenty for wide angle as well. Maybe two dives here is more the order of the day.

It is dubbed the Spaghetti Factory as you can start the dive in from the Yap Corner at a place where a wall of sea whips runs from the channel and up the canyon slope. There are also golden

Crocodilefish

Gray reef shark in Miil Channel

Jack school

gorgonians here that sometime hold longnose hawkfish, always a photo favorite.

Swimming into the channel. the walls of this canyon become vertical with plenty of cracks and crevices creating beautiful light shows. There are soft corals in many of the small caves and cuts and yellow tubastrea corals with bright polyps. Look on these tubastreas for parasitic nudibranchs or Wentletrap snails that mimic the color and bore into these corals. They make good macro subjects.

At the first point here there is a huge rock in the center of the channel. It is a cleaning station where sharks line up to be preened by small, fearless wrasse fish. They will open their mouths to let the wrasse in while trying to stay somewhat static with a swishing tail. This rock also has a large bigeye jack school on occasion.

Diving at the mouth of Miil can provide the diver with the opportunity to see the mantas and lots of other fish as well. The best time to dive here, which can be about a 45 minute swim to the Manta Ridge, is at incoming tide.

Take your time on this dive and look in all of the holes and around the corals. You will see big moray eels, crocodilefish waiting for prey and shimmering schools of pyramid

Sharpnose barracuda

butterflyfish. Whitetip sharks commonly sleep on the channel bottom. Sea turtles also graze along the wall or move along the channel bottom.

The vastness of this channel is truly humbling. There are not many places like this in the ocean world that can be casually dived and explored in clear, blue water.

11) Manta Ridge
Location: Mill Channel
Attractions: Manta Rays, lots of fish
Depth: 25 to 90 feet
Level: Snorkel, advanced, pro

Located in the Miil Channel, this site is guaranteed to provide high voltage diving action. Manta Ridge has been dubbed such because divers can just about be assured of seeing a manta either pass by or stop to feed or get cleaned when diving here.

Manta Ridge itself is a shallow rise across the channel that rises to as shallow as 25 feet. This make the current build and roll over it on incoming tide. This attracts a lot of different fish. The formation leading to the ridge creates a fork, with a deep canyon on the left and the slope going up to the ridge on the right.

In the deeper canyon, as many as 60 juvenile gray reef sharks hang in shallow water, circling in the box canyon. The sharks are curious and come in close for divers to see. There is always a large school of bigeye jacks somewhere in the area. Sometimes they are at the front of the fork. Sometimes they move over the Ridge or near the box canyon area.

Larger sharks also circle along the walls of this canyon near the Ridge, and a morning sun brings clear sunlight basking rays down upon the menacing looking but curious sharks.

When the tide is strong, divers can use reef hooks and hook in to see what the dive will bring. There are times the

Soft corals

diver will blow like a flag in the breeze if the tide is running around the full moon. But this usually brings plenty of fish action.

While the visibility in here is at times low at outgoing tide, that is why the mantas are here, to feed on the nutrients in the water. Red and black snappers hang in loose schools at the base of the pinnacle and sea whips flow with the current. Near the sea whips on the channel side of the ride is a rock with glassfish and usually many leaf fish. Eagle rays also like the outgoing tide and sometime come around in schools of up to 14 rays.

Even if the mantas don't show up, or if they just pass through, don't be disappointed. Take a good look around this ridge. It is bursting with activity. I have had large parrotfish come and start nibbling coral just feet away from my vantage point. Grey reef and whitetip sharks pass by all the time. There is a gorgeous anemone here with shocking purple tips and skunk clownfish. Green moray eels are found in some of the holes on the ridge. The relatively shallow depth allows a lot of bottom time that gives the diver plenty of time for observation. Take advantage of this opportunity to watch Mother Ocean's creatures firsthand.

Nutrients are carried by the currents from the mangroves to the sea, which is great for marine life but bad for visibility. High, slack tide means clears water, little or no current and ease of swimming. With incoming tide you can also drift from the ridge back into the channel to check some of the cleaning stations and other coral gardens.

After a short swim up the left side of the wall, a sloping area appears that holds large hard coral formations. During mating season, the mantas like to chase one another in the open water off this elbow in the channel.

Bluespotted grouper

Deep Cleaning area

12) Deep Cleaning Station
Location: Miil Channel
Attractions: Garden eels, gorgonians, and mantas
Depth: 20 to 95 feet

Located far up the Miil Channel, toward the islands, this is a short swimming to a very pretty area of snow white sand dotted with rocks that serve as a cleaning station for manta rays.

Divers normally swim at 40 to 60 foot depths here, observing coral on the left and whatever decides to swim up the channel. Soon, the diver arrives at a long, sloping bank with tons of red and golden gorgonians on it that starts in about 25 feet and cascades down past 70. The gorgonians have snowy, white polyps. They probably thrive on the outfall from another smaller channel that spills into Miil here. Some have a light silt covering. These gorgonians are found in the more turbid water of harbors and channels but are nice to look at nevertheless.

Following them down the sloping wall to sand bar at 70 feet. Here, sand spills into the channel, forming a plain landscaped with white sand, corals, fans and small baitfish. Watch your breathing and settle down to ground level. The observant diver will see the garden of small eels. These animals like current-swept, sandy places. They live individually in burrows from which they pop out to feed on plankton. From

Manta in shallow water

Emperor angelfish

area. And one interesting sidelight, there is a stone money piece in channel. How it got there is unknown. There are also individual large bumphead parrotfish, lots of small baitfish on acropora corals and even an occasional turtle. Eagle rays also come by in the channel. Sea anemones abound here. Also, there are many hard corals and sea whips near the Manta Ridge. Lots of big, green cup coral stands sit along channel. This coral thrives where there is a good current. Also, keep an eye out for lone large snappers.

13) Stammitsch
Location: Mill Channel
Attractions: Manta Rays, lots of fish
Depth: 15 to 70 feet

a distance, they might look like a carpet of sea grass swaying in the breeze. It is easy to miss them as they completely disappear if alarmed. They don't like bubbles, so take shallow breaths and exhale slowly. Whitetip sharks sleep in the area as well.

It's a great spot for macro or wide angle work. There are lots of fish in

Found in the last year by Yap Diver's Alex Raimon, this place is an amazing spot to watch manta rays and all kinds of fish life. Alex saw wing tips of mantas near the surface in a reefy area far back into Miil Channel. Prior to

Clownfish at the New Cleaning Station

this discovery, this area was not a dive site. Now it is called Stammitsch, a German word for a special meeting table.

What Alex found was a long, loaf shaped reef running from a shallow 12-15 feet along the top and cascading down into a deep channel at one end. Manta swim the length of the coral encrusted formation, stopping at a huge expanse of beautiful yellow finger corals that is a huge cleaning area for many kinds of fish but is dominated by the mantas when they are there. It is large enough as many as five mantas can move around getting preened by cleaner wrasses at one time.

About the only drawback is that it is far into the lagoon and visibility can be a bit milky at times. But the mantas seem to be curious about divers and manage to approach closely. So getting a nice manta photo here is a given.

This site also has a lot of fish life. Look for queen angels, parrotfish, sea turtles and lots to tomato clownfish.

Stammitsch reeftop and mantas

14) Gofnuw Channel
Location: Northeast Yap
Attractions: Manta Rays, fish schools
Depth: 20 to 80 feet

The Miil Channel has become synonymous with observing manta rays, but they don't frequent that channel as often during the months between June and October as they do the rest of the year. It was found they migrate to Gofnuw Channel on the northeast coast during these months. There is not a ridge as there is in Miil, but there is mound that rises to about 60 feet that has some large coral heads nearby. The currents flow around these big heads and

Kayaking the Yap mangroves

Cleaning station at Slow & Easy

over the mound and the mantas seem to enjoy feeding and swimming here.

The rest of this channel is good to dive as well, and again, it is best at slack, high tide to get optimum visibility, which is about 60 to 80 feet. On a drift in, look for moray eels, sleeping leopard sharks and whitetips, marble rays and some very nice sea anemones. There are various hard corals, especially on the coral heads in the channel center, that have cleaner wrasse. There is also a large coral head at the side of the channel near the moorings that are the favored cleaning areas. Outgoing tide and slack tide are both good times to see mantas in this area. Look or nudibranchs and sea moths here too.

15) Slow & Easy
Location: North east Yap
Attractions: Mandarinfish
Depth: 5 to 100 feet

This is a wonderful site for many types of diving and photography. As the name implies, this is the kind of dive where there is no rush. As one of the best macro sites in Yap, underwater photographers will enjoy choosing a depth and just cruising along with your guide or even on your own to see just what is there.

The dive is in the main channel close to Colonia, so a short boat ride gets you plenty of time to look around. The dive can start at the close mooring or the one more toward the channel. The dive is normally done from mooring to mooring. The dive from the close mooring goes through a coral garden that goes out to a point with some beautiful coral formations.

The terrain then changes and becomes a sandy slope with scattered corals and lot of big bommies in the upper reaches in shallow water.

There is a resident hawksbill turtle that can be usually found sleeping or loping around the more coraline part of the dive. These corals also hold cleaning stations that have a variety of cleaner shrimp from hingebeaks to scarlet lady to barber shop shrimp. Also, look under the underhangs of the corals for nudibranchs. This place is very good for a variety of nudis.

Look for various signal gobies and their blind shrimp keeping their holes clean in the sandy slope. Odd pipefish like the stick pipefish and harlequin ghost pipefish are seen here well-camouflaged (another reason to tak it slow). Striped and fantail pipefish also make homes in the corals.

An occasional manta ray, big stingray or shark will swim by, but this spot is mostly for your little stuff. Sea moths like the sand as well. Look and you will be rewarded as well as surprised.

16) Rainbow Reef - O'Keefe's Island
Location: North east Yap
Attractions: Mandarinfish
Depth: 0 to 20 feet

Traditionally dressed Yapese ladies at sunset

Mating mandarinfish

A new addition to the diving aside from the ever-popular Slow & Easy is Rainbow Reef. It is also a short trip from the town and features tons of cardinalfish, beautiful mandarinfish and an old shipwreck of unknown origin. This site is in the mangroves near the island of the famous stone money importer David O'Keefe.

This is normally done as a dusk dive and features mating mandarinfish, some of the most colorful creatures on the reef. As the sun goes down, the males get randy and the pursuit of females is an almost nightly event. The pairs will swim together into the water column to release sperm and eggs and some amazing photo opportunities exist to finish off the day.

As it is dark and mandarinfish don't hold still very much, they aren't easy photo subjects. Try to not shine your light directly on them when waiting for a couple to pair up and go for it. Shield the bean of your light and try to follow them clandestinely. When they start heading up into the water column, then they are rapt and don't care, then you can shine your light and fire away.

But there are other things to see in this oddball inner bay world. Castle corals and tons of cardinalfish inhabit the shallows. If you swim don to about 80 feet, you will find an old copper plated shipwreck. There is no upper structure on this ship but there is some coral growth and a nice cleaning station near the area where the ship touches the reef.

In the shallows, look for seahorses too. One doesn't even need to dive here to see a lot. It is a nice afternoon snorkel excursion and you can also go onto O'Keefe's Island, which is a kind of a local park, and see the remnants of the foundation of his home.

Palau's Southwest Islands

Palau also has some isolated islands to the south of its archipelago called the Southwest Islands. These islands are rarely visited. When seas are calmer in the summer, live aboards like the Palau Aggressor have been known to venture down for a bit of an adventure. The people who live here speak a language more like the outer island Yapese people. Fishing and subsistence is the way of life here and there are no hotels or commercial facilities of any sort. Permission by the various island chiefs must be granted in advance to dive or fish here.

Helen Reef is an amazing place. It is a sea bird sanctuary that has a ranger station with three or four Palauans staying on the island to protect the resources of the 20-mile long atoll. The reef has a large inner passage that is great for diving.

Soft corals at Helen Reef

Helen Reef shipwreck

Diving at the channel mouth on either side when there is a tide change produces a look at many fish, a colorful upper reef and an amazing wall, especially on the left side of the channel. Large gorgonian fans, fields of soft corals and lots of cracks and crevices make for beautiful diving here. The upper reef is also nice with big stands of healthy table corals spread across a broad reef flat.

The upper reef is covered in color anthias, many types of sea anemones and hard corals. The "Nemo" clownfish is found here as it is close to Indonesian and Philippine waters. This type of anemonefish is not found on the northern archipelago. There are a few ominous shipwrecks scattered along the outer reef that have become homes and nesting areas for sea birds like boobies. The ranger station is also covered in birds and is an interesting sand spit to wander around.

Soft coral growing in gorgonian fan at Helen Reef

Yap's Outer Caroline Islands

The people of the outer islands of Yap State, known as the Outer Caroline Islands, have a legendary history of open ocean navigation. They use only natural guides like the stars and the movement of the waves to tell them how to travel vast distances in large outrigger canoes. Most of these islands are atolls or single limestone outcroppings in a vast sea of blue in the northwest-central Pacific ocean. Here an amazing culture has developed where the people are one with the sea. Populations on the islands are not great and they get supplies from Yap central via ship only a few times every year. So they have learned to survive using the sea and the land.

Divers rarely come to visit. Occasionally a small cruise ship, live aboard or sailing ship will call on the islands and divers can thrill to the clear waters and big sharks.

Navigator canoe at Woleai Atoll

Outer island ladies sitting dance

Soft corals at Ngulu

gorgonians dot the walls and large and overly curious (even territorial) silvertip sharks come to see who is invading their space.

On land, visitors are normally welcomed and a visit can be a good reason for dance and celebration. The dances are colorful affairs with chants telling of past island history.

The Chuuk-based dive live aboard Thorfinn occasionally schedules summer trips from Chuuk to Yap or Chuuk to Pohnpei. If a chance presents itself, divers can see a special and isolated culture on land and some varied marine life under the waves.

Diving in a place like Ulithi can produce a look at hundreds of mating sea turtles that show up every summer in the atoll's southern Turtle Islands. Tiger sharks often follow this migration as well as other predators. Dropoffs can be a bit sparse until one reaches the depths where fields of

Ulithi Atoll

Hard corals and snorkeler in Miil Channel

Palau's Ngaardmau Falls

Kaday Village girl making mwarmwars

Saltwater crocodile

Traditional Yap tattoo patterns

Made in the USA
San Bernardino, CA
05 February 2017